RURAL POVERTY IN INDIA

About the Author

B.C. Mehta, formerly Professor of Economics, M.L. Sukhadia University, Udaipur and Emeritus Professor, JNV University, Jodhpur and visiting fellow at University of Pennsylvania, U.S.A. He has published more than 100 research papers in learned journals and twenty books.

Rural Poverty in India

B.C. Mehta
Professor, Department of Economics
Sukhadia University, Udaipur

CONCEPT PUBLISHING COMPANY PVT. LTD.
NEW DELHI-110059

ISBN: 978-81-7022-432-7

Edition 2025

Published and Printed by

Concept Since 1974

Concept Publishing Company Pvt. Ltd.
A/15-16, Commercial Block, Mohan Garden,
New Delhi-110059 (India)
T: 91-11-41101460
E: publishing@conceptpub.com, *W*: www.conceptpub.com

PREFACE

During the past two decades the pervasive nature of rural poverty as well as the limitations of generalised development strategies in poverty alleviation became widely recognised. The issues of agrarian relations and rural development and poverty are now recognised as of fundamental importance but these have been largely ignored in theoretical as well as statistical analysis and in quantitative analysis as well as qualitative probings. In this study, an attempt is made to fill this gap.

Though the enormous short-term fluctuations in the number of rural people suffering from absolute poverty, howsoever defined and measured, needs intensive probing, the focus of this study is on the substantial differences in the level and nature of poverty between states/regions. These differences provide an opportunity for understanding the geophysical, demographic, historical and structural causes of poverty.

When the proposals for this study were submitted to the ICSSR no study of its kind at regional level had been published. Even now most of the studies are confined to regression analysis, mostly either at state level or micro-level. Moreover, study of each region, specially on the basis of the nature of agrarian structure, has not been attempted till now. Hence, it is hoped that this study provides a new insight into the nature of poverty in different regions of the country treating each region to be having more or less a unique poverty experience. The study is diagnostic in nature, it attempts to identify the structural specificity of each region or group of regions and to relate this to its poverty paradigm.

Though the study starts with the usual calorie based measure of poverty, it makes significant departures and builds up seventeen indicators of absolute and relative poverty grouped into four categories : nutritional inadequacy, income insufficiency, resource deprivation and low quality of life. Instead of constructing one or more composite indicators of poverty, profile of each region in terms of its poverty characteristics is prepared. Relatively homogeneous clusters of regions are identified on the basis of these profiles.

Since the analysis is conducted on the basis of the hypothesis that the nature of poverty can be understood only in relation to the nature of the rural economic relations, indicators of agrarian and rural relations are developed and the regions are grouped on the basis of these relations.

Regression exercise is also undertaken to explain the regional differences in the conventionally defined indicators of poverty.

A feature of the work is that it concentrates effort on obtaining an understanding of the nature of poverty in the regions in the light of the relation between poverty and the structure of agrarian relations. Consideration of policy alternatives is touched upon only marginally. That task is left to the users of this research study. Making of policy suggestions would have required going into an indepth study of the strategies and programmes of rural poverty alleviation in operation in the different states till date. This is, clearly, beyond the scope of this study.

In a study of this kind, adequate support from research staff is essential for its success. Dr. Trilok Sharma worked efficiently as Research Associate for most of the duration of the research work. He took great pains in collecting district and region level data from numerous sources, in processing them, and in preparing about 100 indicators of poverty, geophysical, developmental, demographic and structural aspects. Computation of various indicators of poverty was also handled by him. He was helped by Sunil Dalal and Rajni Mathur, specially in the preparation of the standardised scores and composite indicators and running regressions both at the state and region levels. Sunanda Devpura, Hansa Maloo and Divya Mehta helped in filling-in the gaps.

The NSSO refused access to unpublished region-level household expenditure data for the 32nd round of NSS after agreeing to do so. Obviously, availability of these data would have made the research study more useful.

Needless to say, I owe much to all my co-workers in the project. I acknowledge with thanks their excellent support to me in successfully executing it. I am, however, solely responsible for any errors and omissions still present in the study. I am thankful to the ICSSR for giving generous financial support to the study.

B.C. MEHTA

CONTENTS

LIST OF TABLES

INTRODUCTION

Need for the Study

Tackling the problem of poverty specially in rural areas has gained urgency in recent years. Various policy-mixes are being tried out, yet the problem seems nowhere near solution. It is felt that for tackling the problem effectively it is essential to understand the extent and nature of the problem of poverty and its correlates not only at the all India and State levels, as has been done uptill now, but also at as low a level of disaggregation as is permitted by the availability of data. In this context obtaining clear and concrete knowledge of the structural parameters of rural life is indispensable. In the present work we are taking the study to the level of the region as defined by the NSS in its surveys and by the RBI in its Rural Debt and Investment Surveys.

Approaches to Poverty

The different approaches to the problem of poverty in India and the developing countries can be classified into three broad categories: (i) structural, (ii) developmental, and (iii) egalitarian.

The focus in the *structural approach* is on the causes of poverty. Though the debate on the mode of production in Indian agriculture is still inconclusive, it is generally maintained that further expansion of the forces of production and transformation of production relations is checked by the existing property relations and the wrong strategies of agrarian development. The key, therefore, lies with radical change in property relations and the development and extension of class and scale neutral technologies and infrastructural facilities. This, of course, is to be done within the present political framework.

According to this approach, poor is not an economic class. Poverty is the common outcome of a variety of economic relationships and circumstances. Hence categorisation of poor and the non-poor is operationally not relevant. The relevant question is about the cause of poverty, underemployment and low productivity, low wages, unequal exchange and, in general, exploitation. The remedies, therefore, cannot be in terms of the poor identified as such, but in the transformation of the production relations, which cause the phenomenon (Sen 1977: 246-54). Thus, the argument which stresses poverty as a structural process, does not accept the conventional poverty measures.

In contrast to this structural approach to poverty, the second approach can be termed as *developmental approach*. There are many variants of this approach too. However, there is one thing in common, the concern with historical and structural causes of poverty is minimal (Kurien 1977: 6-7). The existing socio-economic structure is, therefore, a datum. It is argued that since rapid rate of growth reduces inequalities and poverty after a time lag (Srinivasan and Bardhan 1974: 393-396), the strategy of development in India should also be that of maximisation of the rate of growth of domestic product.[1] This was, in fact, the strategy of development in the initial phase of planning in India but was reversed latter. This approach also does not need a concrete measure of poverty.

In the third approach, the focus is neither on the structural and institutional causes of poverty nor on the strategy of development and the choice of appropriate technologies but attention is paid to the problems of specific backward regions, sectors and groups of the poor. This approach, therefore, attempts direct and immediate attack on poverty. At present, this seems to be the most popular approach. It does necessitate use of a poverty measure. The poverty measurement studies, besides measuring poverty, have also attempted to identify the characteristics of the poor and to find correlation of poverty with the hypothesised causative factors.

Study of Agrarian Structures

In the last forty-five years various attempts have been made to change the agrarian structure of India. Land reforms legislation has been enacted with varying degrees of success in implementation in different states. Many strategies and policy-packages have been tried to accelerate the growth of output and productivity in agriculture. All these policies and programmes have been superimposed on different regional agrarian structures inherited from pre-independence India.

This has resulted in a much more complex regional agrarian pattern and structure than the one prevailing at the time of independence. In the context of these regional diversities, it has now been realised that the future plans and programmes will have to be region-specific. There have, however, been only few systematic studies of regional structures. Most of the studies have been either too aggregative taking state as the basic unit and discussing mode and relations of production at level or the studies have been very disaggregative, confined to few villages. Though the utility of these studies cannot be doubted and the micro-level studies have indeed helped in clearing many conceptuaı issues regarding rural economy, yet they do not provide enough information and understanding to be helpful to planners. We plan to move in the direction of filling this gap.

Different aspects of agrarian structure in India have been discussed and analysed from different angles. These have helped in understanding the problems of rural poverty. Utsa Patnaik (1972, 1976, 1978, 1980), Paresh Chattopadhyaya (1972), Dipanker Gupta (1980), Ranjit Sau (1976, 1980), A. Rudra (1974, 1978), H.P. Pradhan (1973), Amit Bhaduri (1973), Ghosh and Dutta (1977), Bardhan (1970, 1984), Beteille (1974), Foster-Carter (1978) and others have developed the marxist approach to the mode and relations of production,[2] thus developing the understanding of the stratification of the rural population in India as a whole and in some of the States in particular. Data relating to some villages and other local units selected either purposively or randomly have been collected and examined by many scholars in order to clarify issues involved regarding the existing and emerging structure of the rural economy in parts of the country from the above angle (marxist) and also from the non-marxist point of view. Breman (1974), Pradhan (1976, 1979), Ashok Rudra (1978), Shanin (1977), Mehta (1979, 1980, 1980 II), John Harris (1987), Mehta and Prashad (1988), Mehta and Khandelwal (1981), Vyas N.N. (1980) have attempted such studies. Biplab Das Gupta (1971), K.L. Sharma (1975), B.C. Mehta (1975), Adams and Bumb (1973, 1978), Kundu (1981) and Raza and Kundu (1980) have applied purely statistical techniques such as factor analysis and cluster analysis for identifying different regional structures for some states and, in some cases, India as a whole. This has also been done by some official and semi-official agencies (Registrar General of India, Pandey Committee, N.S.S., RBI, All India Rural Debt and Investment Survey). Changes have been suggested by the Economic Advisory Council of the Prime Minister. Pranab Bardhan (1983, 1984, 1986) has recently made studies of meaningful relations at the regional level.

The present study attempts to make an advance on these approaches and tries to develop an understanding of the agrarian structure of different regions on the basis of variety of indicators, different combinations of which are hypothesised to lead to different economic structures. The different indicators are examined in relation to each other and a typology of regions is developed on the basis of these combinations. In most of the previous studies attempts were made to extract common factors from multitude of variables and then to classify the regions on the basis of the strength of these common factors. In contrast, the focus of the present study is on the implications of these different combinations and on understanding the structures on the basis of differences rather than common factors. The problem of poverty is studied in relation to these structures.

Measurement of Poverty and Correlates

While the structural approach to poverty is adopted in this study and structural profiles of the regions are prepared, as a supplementary study, appropriate measures of poverty are also developed. Though these traditional and new measures of poverty cannot explain the structural processes of poverty generation, and do not even represent poverty in a unique and unambiguous way, these do provide important information about the socio-economic conditions of the poor. Moreover, without developing these indicators and using them in combination with the structural variables, the deficiency in measuring and depicting poverty cannot be brought out fully. Thus, various poverty indicators are used, here not as criteria for policy-decisions but as representing, various parts of the reality. A full chapter is, therefore, devoted to the development of appropriate measures of poverty, if poverty is to be measured at all.

Though the structural approach to poverty does not accept any quantitative measure of poverty and, therefore, relating any such indicator with the structural variables is unacceptable, still such an exercise is undertaken as a supplementary study so that nutritional inadequacy or income insufficiency are understood in relation to the economic structures of the regions. For this purpose, regression analysis is conducted. Of course, this transfers the hypothesis of correlated characteristics of poverty groups to a hypothesis of correlated characteristics of regions with similar poverty magnitudes. This may not be true in a country of continental dimensions like India. This is, however, a general problem of estimating relations based on cross-sectional approach by cross-regional regressions. The underlying processes in each region are generally different. The parameters estimated from a cross-region regression cannot unravel these in entirety. This limitation is inherent in all such studies and is not specific to this study. While interpreting the results this fact has to be kept in mind.

Objectives

The study aims:

(i) To assess alternative measures of the extent and nature of poverty, study their inter-correlations and develop a set of appropriate indicators of poverty;
(ii) To prepare poverty profiles of all the regions in India on the basis of different indicators of poverty including indicators of quality of life;
(iii) To study causal relations between the traditional measures of poverty and their correlates;
(iv) To study the agrarian structure on the regional level specially in relation to agrarian relations pertaining to land ownership, distribution of assets, labour, credit and produce market conditions etc.;
(v) To develop the indicators of other correlates of poverty and agrarian structure especially related to geo-physical conditions, demographic characteristics, development of infrastructure, use of science and technology, level and growth of agricultural productivity and other variables;
(vi) To understand the rural poverty situation and its dynamics in each region on the basis of its agrarian structure and other correlates of poverty; and
(vii) To prepare a typology of rural poverty and its correlates.

Methodology[3]

Basically, the method followed consists in grouping variables into geo-physical, demographic, infrastructural development, land relations, rural labour market, credit market, production and productivity in agriculture and level of economic development and related aspects. Regions are ranked by the clustering measures on each group, in many cases a numerical value is assigned, but in others, regions are simply typed, without any presumption, necessarily, that a particular region type was conducive or not conducive to agricultural growth. While some of the environmental variables like rainfall, can be treated as exogenous, most of the input variables and their composite indicators are interdependent. Even growth in agricultural output would in turn influence demand for health services, infrastructural investments, and the like.

Our underlying framework is that it will be particular combinations of variables that are important, so that, say, certain tenancy arrangements will only prove detrimental to agricultural growth and poverty eradication when observed in combination with certain indebtedness patterns, but the indebtedness pattern may exist with the tenancy relationship without detriment to output, and *vice-versa*, so that the richness of the interrelationship would not be captured by conventional multiple regression and/or simultaneous equations approaches. In fact, such approaches may look promising by the criteria of goodness of fit, but this may gloss over the particular structures of individual regions. Since our objective is to formulate policies appropriate to the varieties of natural history, and colonial and post-independence experience of quite different regions, it is important to develop a framework that treats each region as more than just an observation in some average relationship. We anticipate that the combination of our indicators will reduce to a relatively small number so that it will be possible to meaningfully speak of typology of regional agrarian structures and their correlation with poverty.

A study of agrarian structure and relating it to growth pattern and poverty helps not only to explain why and how the pattern has emerged but also to indicate the most likely pattern in future. Identification of some specific growth patterns may help in understanding the structural causes of stagnation and growth in contrast to the purely environment and resource based factors. In addition, this may throw light on the question: Why different regions having similar environment-resource endowment have responded and developed differently? This may also tell us why the same stimuli may lead to altogether different development experiences in the future.

The reply to questions like why things happened as they have and why they have not happened as desired, why different growth patterns emerge out of similar policy mixes and similar other questions cannot be obtained with the help of the existing statistical tools. The method adopted by us helps us in identifying the similarities and divergences of different growth experiences and, consequently, in suggesting broadly differential policy packages.

The method can be summarised as follows:

(i) Assessment of different norms used for measuring poverty, development of appropriate indicator/indicators of poverty from NSS and other sources;

(ii) Development of indicators representing different aspects of agrarian structure and other correlates of poverty;

(iii) Development of hypotheses regarding the derivation of a particular agrarian structure from a particular combination of variables and the consequences flowing therefrom specially in relation to the problem of poverty;

(iv) Each variable or composite indicator developed from closely related variables is standardised;

(v) In each group of variables (say, labour market), each region is ranked in accordance with each significant variable and the profile of the region is read horizontally in the table of rankings e.g. in a particular region the percentage of agricultural labour in workforce may be high, most of them may be attached labourers, landless or with little land, belong to Scheduled Castes and Scheduled Tribes and may be working for wages in cash. Seen in this way, the labour market profile of each region would be distinctly identified;

(vi) Similar profiles are prepared for each of the group of variables for each region;

(vii) All these profiles are then put side by side and read horizontally for each region revealing a particular agrarian structure and the corresponding poverty problem in a particular region;

(viii) Typology of rural agrarian relations and poverty profiles is prepared and the regions classified accordingly;

(ix) Clustering technique is used to divide the regions into groups of similar poverty profiles and agrarian structures; and

(x) Attempts are made to study the relation between the traditional and new measures of poverty and agrarian structure and socio-economic development using multivariate regression analysis.

Indicators

The complete list of indicators is given in the appendices to this chapter. They are divided into the following blocks:

(1) Poverty and Quality of life Variables
(2) Geo-physical Conditions
(3) Infrastructure and Inputs
(4) Production and Productivity in Agriculture
(5) Rural Labour Market
(6) Land Relations
(7) Credit Market
(8) Demographic Characteristics
  (a) Sex-bias
  (b) Urbanisation
  (c) Rural Settlement
  (d) Population Pressure
(9) Socially Oppressed Classes
(10) Miscellaneous Factors

Sources of Data

District level data are collected by different departments of state governments and are published in the state statistical abstracts or reports, departmental reports, plan documents, district gazetteers and other official papers.

Agricultural and economic censuses also provide wealth of data. Census of India 1961 published many series for each district. These and similar studies were conducted for indentifying backward districts. RBI, NSS and other central statistical agencies use different definitions and differ in scope, coverage, period, sampling design and techniques and the quality of the field staff. Care is taken to include only broadly comparable data. Specific sources are indicated at appropriate places.

The main source of data is NSS, 27th round (Oct. 1972–Sept. 1973) household budget data for rural India. As is well known NSS collects data by interview method through a consumer expenditure data schedule. A probability sample is drawn. A stratified multi-stage design is used for selecting households. Two independent and interpenetrating half samples are selected. The divergence between the two half sample estimates gives an estimate of the margin of error involved in the results. Each selected household is interviewed for collecting data on expenditure on all items of consumption during the 'last 30 days' preceding the date of enquiry: (a) Purchases in cash and on credit, (b) receipts in kind or in exchange of goods and services, (c) Home-grown and home-consumed goods, and (d) transfer receipts are included in consumption.

The household consumption expenditure data at regional level have been published only for the 27th round in the NSS publication *Sarvekshana* (1983: s-1 to s-88).

NSS tabulation gives information on distribution of households by expenditure classes. It also gives the per capita expenditure, average per capita calorie intake, the proportion of total expenditure incurred on food items for each of the expenditure classes for rural and urban households separately.

The NSS estimates of per capita consumption expenditure are subject to many errors. In some years these have been overestimates, and in other, underestimates of the actual level of consumption derived from per capita availability of food items.

According to Tyagi, in 1960-61 and 1961-62, the annual per capita consumption of foodgrains in the country was estimated by NSS at 225.7 kg. and 220.7 kg., respectively, as against the availability figures of only 171 kg. for 1969 and 168.2 kg. for 1962. One wonders where from this much foodgrain came as the NSS estimate worked out to be 20 per cent higher than even the "production + imports". The NSS estimates for 1960-61 and 1961-62 were higher than the official estimates of availability by over 30 per cent. And if one were to consider the fact that NSS estimates pertain only to household consumption, while official estimates relate to total availability, the difference would be still larger. Since then, the differences between the two have narrowed down. In 1973-74, according to NSS, the annual per capita consumption of foodgrains was at 185.6 kg. as against officially estimated availability of 164.6 kg. in 1974. This gives a divergence of only 12 per cent. However, such a divergence could arise in the seventies because of some or all of the following reasons: the share of government consumption was larger (i.e. less grain was available for private consumption), stocks held privately by traders and farmers were higher than in the sixties or there was improvement in the coverage and methodology of estimating production (Tyagi 1985: 239).

As against this, Dandekar and Rath found that NSS estimate of per capita consumption for 1967-68 was an underestimate (Dandekar and Rath, 1971).

The whole of India has been divided by the NSS into 66 agro-climatic regions. Regions have been formed by grouping districts (or parts of districts) having similar population density and cropping pattern.

Most of the data are available for districts and not regions. For deriving the relevant information at regional level, districts are assigned to regions as per All India Debt and Investment Survey 1971-72 classification.

Sources of data about the correlates of poverty are much more varied than the above one. Main sources are the Statistical Abstracts of different states, census reports for each state separately, Census of Agriculture, Reserve Bank of India, All India Debt and Investment Survey, data processed and published by many researchers, specially Bhalla and Alagh (1979) and Mahendra Dev (1986). Most of the data are at district level. The absolute numbers for constituent districts are totalled up for each region and then appropriate ratios are calculated.

Note of Caution

There is no doubt that arbitrariness exists in this study. It exists in choosing the variables, in their measurement, and in their grouping. One way of minimising arbitrariness in the selection of variables is to take up as many variables as possible without making serious conceptual and measurement errors and then devise composite indicators of closely related traits and characteristics.

Measurement instruments (e.g. calorie, protein, etc.) for each variable (say, nutrition) are, almost universally, not unique.

Classifying the variables in groups also involves arbitrariness. For example, illiteracy or low education can be classified in Resource

Deprivation or in Quality of Life or in the Correlates of Poverty.

Gutkind (1986: 51-54) includes 73 variables in the micro-level study of the American poor. His list is subdivided into 5 blocks as follows: (I) Demographic variables (9), (II) Economic variables (8), (III) Employment (9), (IV) Quality of life (20), and (V) Subjective variables (27). Data are collected from a field survey.

Since our study is based on regional data, many degrees of freedom are lost, specially data about subjective variables cannot be collected. Of the rest of the variables, we have collected as much information as possible.

Scope of the Study

This study is confined to a study of rural poverty. The study covers all the 64 regions in India. Though state level study for 1972-73 and 1983-84 has also been conducted and results cited at appropriate places, the focus is only on regional study. Regional poverty study is based on NSS data on consumption expenditure thrown up by round number 27 (1972-73).

Chapter Scheme

Since the present state policies are mostly based on one concrete measure of poverty, the complicated problem of defining and measuring poverty is tackled first. The problem involves bringing out all facets of poverty and then conceptualising uni-dimensional or multi-dimensional measures of the same. The problem of choosing an appropriate computational formula for obtaining a summary measure for inter-period, inter-spatial and inter-temporal comparisons and satisfying certain welfare axioms, has also to be solved. These are all discussed in Chapter 2.

Results about the various measures of poverty viz. Head-count ratio, Poverty gap, Sen's Index, per capita expenditure, resource deprivation, inequality in distribution of expenditure, calorie intake and assets, and quality of life are presented in Chapter 3. Their inter-relationships and sensitivity of poverty measure to poverty norm and formula are also examined.

In Chapter 4, the complete poverty profile of each region in terms of the poverty indicators developed in this study is presented and discussed, poverty distance matrix is calculated and cluster of regions with similar poverty profiles are identified.

In Chapter 5, results of regression of the conventional measures of poverty on blocks of geo-physical, infrastructural and other structural correlate are presented. The three measures of poverty chosen are: the composite indicator of nutritional insufficiency, average per capita expenditure and real income.

Since the stress in this study is on obtaining an understanding of the problem of poverty on the basis of the rural economic relations and structures, sets of structural variables are developed in Chapter 6. Structural difference matrix between regions is computed and structural clusters are developed. This is to help in indentifying a poverty typology of agrarian relations.

In the last chapter, results are summarised and general conclusions of the study are derived. A typology of poverty is prepared and complete profiles of regions in terms of poverty measures and closely related geo-physical, demographic and structural variables are presented. Policy implications are also brought out.

NOTES

1. James, Naya and Meier (1988) argue that countries of Asia which stressed growth in place of equity (Newly industrialised countries) achieved greater equality than those countries (in South Asia) which stressed equity over growth.
2. For a summary presentation of the debate, see A. Thorner (1982: 1961-1968, 1993-1999) and K.L. Sharma (1983: 1996-1803, 1851-1855). Papers published in *EPW* have now been brought out in a single volume. See Utsa Patnaik (1990).
3. I am thankful to W.A. Heston for his suggestions.

APPENDIX-I

COMPLETE LIST OF INDICATORS USED IN THIS STUDY

A. Poverty Measures

I *Nutritional Inadequacy* (*1972-73*)

1	UPPL	Poverty line, ultrapoor
2	PPL	Poverty line, poor
3	PUP	Percentage ultrapoor (Head-Count ratio, H)
4	PP	Percentage poor
5a	PG_1	Poverty-gap in terms of expenditure for ultrapoor
5b	PG_2	Poverty-gap in terms of expenditure for poor
5c	PG_3	Poverty-gap in terms of calorie for ultrapoor
5d	PG_4	Poverty-gap in terms of calorie for poor
6a	SI_1	Sen's Index for ultrapoor; expenditure
6b	SI_2	Sen's Index for poor; expenditure
6c	SI_3	Sen's Index for ultrapoor; calorie
6d	SI_4	Sen's Index for poor; calorie
6	SI	Sen's Index, composite index of 6a to 6d
7a	PEF	Percentage outlay on food at ultrapoor poverty line
8	P	Composite Index of Nutritional Poverty (H, PG & SI) or CIP

II *Income Insufficiency and Inequality* (*1972-73*)

9	APE	Average per capita expenditure (in Rs.)
10	RY	Real Income (= APE/UPPL)
11	CY	Concentration of expenditure (a) m, (b) m′ and (c) m_1
12a	LY_1	LR of distribution of calorie in all households
12b	LY_2	LR of distribution of expenditure
12	LY	Composite index of inequality in distribution of expenditure

13a	DAP_1	LR of ultrapoor in terms of distribution of expenditure
13b	DAP_2	LR for ultrapoor in terms of calorie
13c	DAP_3	LR for poor and ultrapoor, expenditure
13d	DAP_4	LR for poor, calorie
13	DAP	Composite indicator of expenditure/calorie inequality among the poor

III *Resource Deprivation*

14a	AVA	Average value of total assets held by rural households as on 1st June 1971
14b	AVLS	Average value of livestock (all RHHs)
14c	AVIM	Average value of equipment (all RHHs)
14	CIA	Composite indicator of assets
15a	$PLAHH_1$ (AD_1)	Percentage of low asset households with assets valued less than Rs. 2500
15b	$PLAHH_2$ (AD_2)	Percentage of low asset households with assets valued less than Rs. 5000
15	AD	Index of asset deprivation
16b	$PLLHH_1$	Percentage of low land households: Percentage of households owning land less than 2.5 acres
16b	$PLLHH_2$	Percentage of low land households: Percentage of households owning land less than 5 acres
16c	ALO	Average land owned per household
16d	POL	Pressure on land — Number of households per 100 acres = 100/ALO
16	LD	Composite index of land deprivation
16d	CA	Concentration of assets
17b	CVLC	Coefficient of variation of land cultivated across size classes
17c	CL	Concentration ratio of land operated
17	COLA	Composite index of concentration of land and assets
18	URR	Rural unemployment rate

IV *Quality of Life*

19	SURR	Survival ratio
20	IMR	Infant mortality rate

21	PKH	Percentage of Kutcha Houses (Rural)
22	FILLR	Female illiteracy rate
23	QOL	Composite quality of life indicator

B. Correlates of Poverty

V *Geo-Physical*

1	NR	Annual normal rainfall
2	DEFRAIN	Percentage deficit of actual Rainfall
3	CRAIN	Proportion of annual normal Rainfall concentrated in June-September monsoon
4	SOIL	Soil Rating

VI *Forces of Production in Agriculture: Infrastructure and Inputs*

5	EP	Number of electric pumpsets and oil engines used per hectare of cropped area in 1971
6	IRR	Percentage area irrigated
7	IWT	Area irrigated from wells and tubewells
8	IC	Intensity of cropping
9	FERT	Value in Rs. of fertilizers used in 1970-71 per hectare of area under 19 major crops averaged over districts in each region
10	CII	Composite indicator of infrastructure and inputs
11	CIA	Composite indicator of assets (capital base)

VII *Agricultural Production*

12	OPC	Output per capita of all crops (1970-73)
13	OPH	Output per hectare of all crops (1970-73)
14	AGR	Average exponential annual growth rate of output of 19 major crops, 1962-65 – 1970-73

VIII *Rural Labour Market*

15	RFL	Regular farm male labour in 15-55 years age-group as proportion to total farm male labour in this age-group
16	URR	Average daily rural unemployment rate, 1972-73

17	WL	Percentage of farm wage labourers in rural labour force in the 15-59 years age-group
18	AWE	Average rate of earning per manday of farm wage-work for males in the 15-59 years age-group in rural non-cultivating wage earner HHs in 1970-71 at 1960-61 prices
19	AgL/CUL	Percentage of agricultural labourers to cultivators
20	LABPROD	Labour productivity (in Rs.) for triennium ending 1964-65.

IX *Land Relations: Leasing Activity*
(All as on June 1, 1971. *Source*: AIDIS, 1971-72)

21	PLO	Percentage of rural households leasing-out land
22	PLOUM	Percentage of HHs leasing-out under usufructuary mortgage
23	PLI	Percentage of households leasing-in
24	PLISC	Percentage of HHs leasing-in for share of produce
25	PALL	Percentage of Rural HHs owning but not operating land (absentee landlords)
26	PLIMF	Percentage of Rural HHs land owned .5 to 2.5 acres leasing-in
27	PLOMF	Percentage of Rural households land owned .5 to 2.5 acres leasing-out (percentage L-O marginal farmers)
29	PLISF	Percentage of rural households land owned 2.5 to 5 acres leasing-in
30	PLIMSF	Percentage of RHHs to total land owned < 5 acres leasing-in
31	PLOMSF	Percentage of RHHs to total land owned < 5 acres leasing-out
32	PLORF	Percentage of rural households owning land more than 7.5 acres leasing-out

X *Rural Debt and Credit Relations*
(All as on June 1, 1971. *Source*: AIDIS, 1971)

32	PDHH	Percentage of deficit households (All RHHs)

33	PDHHAg	Percentage of deficit households-sgricultural labourers (All HHs)
34	DFB	Percentage of debt for farm and non-farm business expenditure (All HHs)
35	DCP	Percentage of debt for household expenditure (All HHs)
36	DFBAgL	Percentage of debt for farm and non-farm business expenditure (Ag. labourers)
37	DCPAgL	Percentage of debt for HH expenditure (Ag. Lab.)
38	DIA	Percentage of debt from financial institutions
39	DLL	Percentage of debt from landlords (All HHs)
40	DAgML	Percentage of debt from Agricultural money-lenders (All HHs)
41	DMPLT	Percentage of debt from professional moneylenders and traders (All HHs)
42	DIAAgL	Percentage of debt by agricultural labourers from institutional agencies
43	DLLAgL	Percentage of debt by agricultural labourers from landlords
44	DAgMLAgL	Percentage of debt by agricultural labourers from agricultural moneylenders
45	DPMLAgL	Percentage of debt by agricultural labourers from professional moneylenders
46	DTAgL	Percentage of debt by Agricultural labourers from traders
47	DAR	Debt asset ratio
48	ADEBT	Average debt on all HHs
49	PIND	Percentage of rural households reporting cash dues outstanding

XI *Demographic Variables, 1971, Census*

(i) *Sex-bias*

50	SR	Sex ratio

(ii) *Settlement of Population*

51	DU	Degree of Urbanisation

52	PSV	Proportion of total inhabited villages in each region having a population of less than 200
53	ASPACE	Average spacing of villages
54	ASV	Average size of villages

(iii) *Population Pressure*

55	gp	Rate of decadal population growth (1961 to 71)
56	DR	Dependency ratio
57	DP	Density of population per square km.
58	PhyD	Physiological density

XII *Social Oppression and Remoteness*

59	SC	Percentage of scheduled castes in total rural male population
60	ST	Percentage of scheduled tribes in total rural male population
61	SCST	Percentage of SC+ST population in total rural male population

XIII *Miscellaneous Factors*

62	NONAG	Proportion of working population in the region in manufacturing, repairing and services, 1971

Sources: S. Mahendra Dev (1986)
P. Bardhan (1986)
Census of India, 1971
Indian Agricultural Statistics,
All India Debt and Investment Survey, 1971-72, R.B.I.

APPENDIX-II

NAME OF REGIONS

Andhra Pradesh

1. Coastal
2. Inland Northern
3. Inland Southern

Assam

4. Plains
5. Hills

Bihar

6. Southern
7. Northern
8. Central

Gujarat

9. Eastern Plains
10. Plains Northern
11. Plains Southern
12. Dry Areas
13. Saurashtra

Haryana

14. Eastern
15. Western
16. *Himachal Pradesh*

J. & K.

17. Outer Hills
18. Jhelum Valley

Kerala

19. Western Northern
20. Southern

Madhya Pradesh

21. Eastern
22. Inland Eastern
23. Inland Western
24. Western
25. Northern

Maharashtra

26. Coastal
27. Inland Western
28. Inland Northern
29. Inland Central
30. Inland Eastern
31. Eastern

Karnataka

32. Coastal and Ghats
33. Inland Eastern
34. Inland Southern
35. Inland Northern

Orissa

36. Coastal
37. Southern
38. Northern

Punjab

39. Northern
40. Southern

Rajasthan
41. Western
42. North Eastern
43. Southern
44. South Eastern

Tamil Nadu
45. Coastal Northern
46. Coastal Southern
47. Inland
48. *Tripura*

Uttar Pradesh
49. Himalayan
50. Western
51. Central
52. Eastern
53. Southern

West Bengal
54. Himalayan
55. Eastern Plains
56. Central Plains
57. Western Plains

Manipur
58. Plain
59. Hills

60. *Meghalaya*
61. *Delhi*
62. *Goa, Daman & Diu*
63. *Pondicherry*
64. *J. & K. Mountainous*

2

MEASUREMENT OF POVERTY

I
INTRODUCTION

The problem of defining and measuring poverty has to be faced squarely for obtaining an understanding of not only the extent of poverty but also its nature without which it is impossible to devise effective policies. However, the measurement problem is not independent of the objectives of this particular study.

The objectives of poverty analysis may be diverse. As for instance:

(a) To estimate the incidence of poverty (i.e., the number of proportion of the population living in poverty).
(b) To identify the poor on the basis of a dividing-line (in terms of income, calorie intake, land owned, caste etc.).
(c) To calculate the magnitude of the poverty problem (e.g., the poverty gap), the income generation required or the transfer of income needed to bring all those who are under poverty above it.
(d) To analyse the characteristics of the poor (e.g. distribution of income or consumption among the poor).
(e) To study the phenomena causing poverty: market exploitation, non-market exploitation, non-exploitative reasons, etc.

The first four need a concept of poverty and a method of measurement of poverty (Ringen, 1985 : 99), while the last one deals with the question of political economy. Here, in this chapter, attention has been confined to the problem of measurement of poverty assuming that this is useful in analysing poverty.

In Section II, the problem of conceptualising and defining poverty is discussed and alternative measures of poverty are developed. The problem of preparing appropriate indicators of poverty are also dealt with in this section.

II
MEASURES OF POVERTY

Stein Ringen (1985 : 99-137) discusses two stages of measurement of poverty. In the first stage, measurement of poverty is defined in relation to minimum necessities: what is necessary to maintain physical health. In the second stage (Rowntree, 1901), poverty is defined in relation to the necessities of social efficiency'.

Thus, the second stage poverty measurement defines poverty in terms of relative deprivation which, of course, is an aspect of the social situation of the poor. But a crucial question arises in this respect: Is income or any other single indicator (e.g. per capita daily calorie intake) an adequate indicator of social situation or welfare of the individuals? Obviously, it is not. Income is only one of the several conditions. Moreover, the connection between income and other components has been found to be low. (Titmus, 1962 Uusitalo, 1975; Ringen, 1985:102).

Ringen argues that the concept of poverty cannot be completely relativised — all persons in a poor country may be poor. Secondly, poverty expresses itself in how people live — people living in want. Only those people who have a low standard of living because they are not able to obtain a higher standard should be considered poor. Hence, poverty has dual aspects:

(i) Conspicuously low standard, and
(ii) Insufficient resources

This situation can be identified as accumulation of deprivation. (Ringen 1985 : 105). Hence, poverty indicators must

(i) be numerous in number
(ii) make it possible to identify deprivation in objective terms, and
(iii) should reflect the resources side as well as the way of life side.

Since income in an inadequate index of welfare, other measures of poverty have to be devised (Hicks, 1982; Lipton, 1983: 4-5). One unidimensional measure is under nutrition. This will necessitate calculation of an adequate level of nutrition. An average person has to be conceptualised and his requirements found out. Generally, the proportion of the population unable to get this much nutrition is to be treated as poor.

After discussing the utilitarian, welfare and Rawlsian approaches, Sen (1983 : 367-369) suggests the basic capability approach to inequality and poverty. Lack of basic capability of basic goods may be because of the shortage of resources *per se* or because of the inequitable distribution of resources which are adequate in supply. Lipton (1983 : 5, 83), therefore, distinguishes between primary poverty due to insufficient resources and secondary poverty which is due to inefficient allocation of resources.[1]

As already pointed out, the concept of poverty arose with the notion of absolute deprivation — failure to provide basic requirements mostly defined in terms of nutritional norms by early observers like Booth (1889) and Rowntree (1901). The basic needs approach is an extension of this approach (Streetan 1981). However, *relative deprivation* is also an essential ingredient of an understanding of poverty. It is suggested that since income is an inadequate measure and any other absolute measure would be arbitrary and static in nature we should drop absolute poverty and opt for relative poverty or relative deprivation. Townsend (1970, 1974), Runciman (1966) and Gutkind (1986) refer to two approaches to 'relative deprivation' or 'relative poverty' : the "objective approach" of conditions of deprivation as given by Townsend (1974) and the 'subjective approach' of feelings of deprivation. Both are, of course, not mutually independent.

Relative deprivation is not the same as 'inequality'. The concept of relative deprivation involves a notion of a *reference group,* the selection of which poses problems. The more different the reference group, the closer is the notion of relative deprivation to inequality (Gutkind, 1986).

However, although poverty and inequality are related and associated issues, they are not identical. Economic inequality cannot capture all the issues (rights, entitlements, exploitation, norms, etc.) embodied in the notion of poverty. In fact, inequality is only one of the factors related to poverty. And, even today the concept of absolute poverty is obviously and depressingly relevant in the developing countries (Sen, 1980; Gutkind, 1986: 27). Inequality of income, which is used to measure relative poverty, can also be a supplementary indicator. It cannot substitute for absolute poverty measure, because, to quote Lipton, "inequality and poverty are different evils" (Lipton, 1983 : 5). What is required, therefore, is an amalgamation of both the absolute and relative considerations (UNO 1954; Sen 1980:3).

Gutkind (1986:28-29) conceptualises poverty as a condition which involves severe 'deprivation, intensified by associated *adverse occurrences* and usually, but not exclusively, associated with inadequate resources. The new concept embodies an element of inequality of income and wealth as well as inequality in opportunities and in access to different markets.

The concept of 'poverty space' can be used to quantify the concept of poverty. This involves the process of 'disaggregation' of the overall concept of poverty.

Different Measures of Poverty

Thus, poverty cannot be treated as a unique category (Gutkind, 1986: 160-161). It can be defined in various ways. These reveal different aspects of poverty. There is no one-to-one correspondence between the alternatives. Poverty can thus be conceptualised as

- Poverty of resources or resource deprivation;
- income insufficiency;
- nutritional deficiency or nutritional deprivation or food inadequacy; and
- poverty in terms of low quality of life.

In all the above four cases, poverty may be considered in absolute or relative terms. We, therefore, consider the following groups of indicators:

1. *Resource Deprivation*

In ordinary parlance when one talks of the rich and the poor, one refers to wealthy and poor persons. Moreover, people earn their livelihood on the basis of either physical and financial capital or human capital. Of course, returns to these forms of capital depend on many factors. The most important factor in the case of human capital is the probability of getting employment. Hence, the following sub-sets of indicators would be used to reflect poverty in terms of resource deprivation:

(i) Physical resource (land and other assets) deprivation;
(ii) Human capital deprivation;
(iii) Rate of unemployment; and
(iv) Measures of inequality in the distribution of land and assets which depict relative poverty.

2. *Income Insufficiency*

Income insufficiency can be considered to be a derivative of resource inadequacy. However, no perfect correlation between the two can be taken for granted. Of course, as against resources income is a flow variable. Income is the basis on which an adequate level of living can be obtained. However, data about income at regional level are not available. Therefore, a proper proxy has to be used. The average per capita consumption expenditure (APE) of households as given by the National Sample Survey (NSS) is the variable chosen. It is also the best proxy for permanent income (Cramer, 1968) on which the consumption pattern is supposed to depend.[2] However, it will be proper to take the real per capita expenditure instead of the nominal per capita expenditure. This is necessary in cross-section studies because there are inter-state differences in consumer prices. Conversion of APE to real income using price indicators has not been attempted here for two reasons: (1) We have not been able to compute appropriate price indices for 63 regions, and (2) it is more appropriate to express real expenditure in terms of calorie norm.[3]

Since we have data about nominal average per capita expenditure (APE) and the expenditure required to attain a calorie norm of say 1920 (UPPL), the ratio of the two will at once give the average expenditure of the region. Thus,

$$RY = APE/UPPL$$

For example, for A.P. region-1 (Coastal), RY will be 39.82/34.25 = 1.1626, since APE = Rs. 39.82 and UPPL = Rs. 34.25. This implies that the nominal APE in A.P. region-1 is just sufficient to provide the dietary energy requirement and other non-food items to 1.1626 persons. This measure abstracts APE from not only price differentials but also the differences in dietary habits and nutritive value of the different items of consumption.

Measures of distribution of income/expenditure are used to

represent relative poverty.

3. *Nutritional Inadequacy (Food Inadequacy)*

This can either be a food based poverty line (Greer and Thorbecke, 1986) or a food adequacy standard of living (Lipton, 1983). The former is defined as the minimum expenditure on food necessary to meet the required dietary allowance of calories, while eating the typical dietary composition of the household (Greer and Thorbecke, 1986: 116). The latter is defined as the total expenditure level (or income level) with which an individual, when left to himself, will meet the calorie need for an active and healthy life (Rao, Gupta and Dutta, 1985: 29; Lipton, 1983:7).[4]

In order to define a food adequacy standard (FAS), which is also a scaler measure, we have to define adequate food or a food norm. Food provides nutrition, calorie, protein, vitamin, etc., which are essential parts of a nutritive diet. However, in order to define a single-scaler poverty indicator, a single component of nutritive diet has to be chosen. This task is made easier because a calorie-adequate diet, especially in Indian conditions and eating habits, is also a protein-adequate diet, whereas the reverse is not always true (Sukhatme, 1977, Lipton, 1983: 8; N.I.N., 1976; McLaren, 1974: 93). In contrast, vitamin inadequacy is unrelated with calorie intake (Berg, 1973). Hence, the calorie indicator is generally chosen as an indicator of food adequacy.[5]

In 1955, FAO/WHO dietary energy requirement (DER) at 10°C or the average reference man was 3200 calorie per day and for an average reference woman it was 2300 calorie (FAO, 1973, 28-31). These have subsequently been reduced several times.

Separate DERs for less developed countries have been prescribed. These are much lower for the less developed countries than the western countries because of differences in climate, weight, height and age-structure (Lipton, 1983:12-25). Nutrition requirements in terms of calorie are age, sex, and occupation specific and, as such, they are likely to vary sizeably between different segments of the population. The Nutrition Expert Group (NEG) has recommended some age-sex-occupation-specific norms. Using appropriate weighting diagram, the daily calorie requirement per person works out, on an average, to around 2400 calories in rural areas and 2100 calories in urban areas. (Planning Commission,

1978-1983:36; Rao, Gupta and Dutta, 1985:30). The Research and Planning Division of ECAFE (1972) estimated the minimum requirement for a person in average health as 2500 calories and 80 protein units.

The assumption of the uniform norm of dietary energy requirement (DER) or norms of calorie requirement has been objected to by many scholars. The main argument hinges on the vast variety of items of food, the very widely different food habits, cooking methods and geoclimatic situations. Sukhatme objects to taking an average nutritional norm for defining poverty because of inter-personal variability of nutritional needs and the existence of adaptive mechanisms in human body (Sukhatme, 1977, 1978: 1373, 1981:1034-36, 1982; Lipton, 1983: 27-34).[6]

Hence, persons eating below or above the average DER are, therefore, not necessarily under or over-nourished. Consequently, classifying people as poor or undernourished in accordance with the average norm when, in fact, they have fully acquired their energy requirements (below average) will create type I error, which is operationally more serious than type II error (of exclusion).

However, Sen reminds us that malnutrition can provide a *basis* for a standard of poverty without poverty being identified as the extent of malnutrition. For example, if 40 per cent of the population is below the poverty line what Sukhatme implies is that the statement is not equivalent to the statement that 40 per cent of the population is under-nourished. Still it is an important statement. It tells us that 40 per cent of the population fails to have incomes adequate for buying enough food items to meet average nutritional requirements. This is definitely an important information (Sen, 1980:4).

For reasons cited above Sukhatme suggests that the numbers at significant risk of under-nutrition equal, roughly, the numbers ingesting below 80 per cent of the average DER (Sukhatme, 1978, 1981; Lipton, 1983:35). The task force (Perspective Planning Division, 1979:7) defines a modest poverty line or reduced poverty line (Planning Commission, 1978:50; 1979:37, at 75 per cent of poverty line. In contrast, the Perspective Planning Division (1962:13-14) had suggested that it should be raised as development goes apace.

Following Lipton and Sukhatme, those who cannot afford this norm, that is 80 per cent of DER level of calorie intake, are termed 'ultra poor' and those able to afford 80 per cent but not 100 per cent of this requirement as 'poor'. In our case the DERs are 2400 calories for the rural poor and 1920 (80% of 2400) for the rural ultra poor, respectively.[7] We define the ultra poor poverty line and poverty line on the basis of these energy norms. As we have already seen, poverty line is defined as the per capita household expenditure level in which an individual, when left to himself, will meet the calorie requirements. This expenditure, besides satisfying the minimum energy requirements (along with other nutritional requirements) also satisfies the minimum non-food needs. However, the minimum non-food requirements vary according to topography, climate, nature, type and intensity of economic activities, etc. One hypothesis is that a person who is able to obtain minimum dietary requirements with his or her income is *ipso facto* assumed to have satisfied the minimum non-food requirements also.[8] Thus, the Planning Commission considers the vector of non-food items of poverty norm class as adequate without any examination.

As is clear from the above discussion, practical measurement of the nutritionally poor would require the nutritionally adequate food bundles of different groups.

The translation of minimum nutritional requirements into minimum food requirements depends on the choice of commodities by the individuals, which, of course, reflects consumer habits and preferences. Moreover, as Gutkind (1986:25) points out, the nutrients required can be seen as an 'input' in a physical, biological process (a production function) which produces health. However, the twin processes of transformation of consumption into nutrition and nutrition into health are not entirely clear. The ambiguity is revealed by nearly no correlation between the nutritionally defined poverty ratio and infant mortality rate of expectation of life. In fact, Kerala has got a very high proportion of nutritional deficiency, however, it has also got a very high expectation of life at birth. This implies that the physical and biological process of transformation of nutrition into health of the Keralaites is much more efficient than the inhabitants of other states. Thus, as has been pointed out repeatedly, the nutrition based poverty ratio may be an inadequate measure of the quality of life.

Lipton thinks that persons/households should spend at least 25 per cent of outlay on non-food requirements, which is the same as saying that not more than 80 per cent of the total outlay be spent on food items. This may be scaled down to 70 per cent if the relative prices of food items decline. Following Lipton, we also adopt a "two-80 per cent" classification of ultra poverty, i.e., the households who spend 80 per cent or more than 80 per cent of outlay on food, but still have below 80 per cent of energy requirements, are considered to be the ultra poor. In fact, we calculate these two indictors separately.

Computation of Nutrition Based Indices of Poverty: Formula Used

Different indicators of poverty, ranging from simple percentages to highly complicated formulae, have been suggested from time to time. Complications arise because equity aspects are also considered. For this, certain axioms may have to be satisfied.[9] Some of the widely used indicators are: (i) The Head-count Ratio, (ii) Poverty Gap, (iii) Sen's Index and (iv) the Lorenz Ratio.

Many experts have worked on Sen's index and modified it mostly by changing the normalisation rule or the weights.

Sen's index and its variants satisfy the criteria (axioms) almost fully. However, these also do not satisfy the strong transfer axioms, and are discontinuous and indecomposable (Kundu, 1981). Kundu's index is based on the coefficient of variation and Thiel index in the place of Gini Coefficient. (Kundu, 1981). Pal and Chakravarti (1985:11) suggest a decomposable index and Foster, Greer and Thorbecke (FGT) (1984) a number of decomposable severity indices. Ravillion and Huppi (1991) use the FGT class of measures. Jain (1987) suggests his own indicators, based on the relative distance weight approach to poverty measurement.

However, Smith and Kundu (1983) have shown that it is impossible to have a poverty measure satisfying all axioms. In this situation it would be better to have several single-dimension measures of poverty, separating absolute and relative measures, rather than developing composite indicators, so that different dimensions of poverty can be studied separately. Also, most of these complex poverty indicators are highly correlated with the simple head-count ratio (Panda, 1987).[10] Hence, empirically there is nothing much to choose between the simple head-count ratio and the more complex indicators. Thus, the head-count ratio can be used to measure absolute nutritional poverty in most of the studies without loosing much in precision. This is especially true in the context of the quality of Indian data. To insist on axiomatic refinements in the context of a poor data base will be a luxury in the Indian situation. In fact, concentration of effort on axiomatic refinements will only divert attention from the basic questions regarding poverty (Dandekar, 1981:1241).

On putting Jain's poverty measures to correlation analysis, it has been found that the various inequality measures like the Gini Coefficient (G), Within Group Inequality (GL) and Normative Inequality measures suggested by Jain (1987) are also highly inter-correlated. However, their correlation with the poverty measures is very weak. Again, the average consumption of population (PU) does not exhibit high correlation with either of the two sets of variables (inequality and poverty). It is, however, interesting to note that on the one hand, states having high per capita expenditure exhibit low poverty and, on the other, they have large inequalities.

Thus, the measure of inequality, poverty and average expenditure represent different aspects of poverty. Hence, in place of the multitude of nutrition-based indicators of poverty, suggested by Sen, Kakwani, Jain and others, it is suggested that only three indicators of poverty will suffice in most of the studies:

(i) The head-count ratio which is the easiest to compute, comprehend and apply in policy-making. Lipton takes the Two-Eighty per cent criterion — The head-count ratio in conjunction with per cent expenditure on food;
(ii) The Lorenz ratio for measuring inequality; and
(iii) The per capita consumption expenditure.

However, in order to test whether the above results still hold in the case of regions, we have computed most of these measures. This will also help us to test the sensitivity of poverty measurements to the choice of norms and formulae.

4. *Low Quality of Life (QOL)*

A measure of the overall basic needs of social goods satisfaction is the physical quality of life index as suggested by Morris (1979). Morris computed the composite index by giving equal weights to life expectancy at age 1, the survival chances from birth to age 1, and adult literacy rate.[11, 12] In our case, in order to correlate with poverty these indicators have to be reversed. He found great divergence in this indicator and per capita income in most Indian states. However, Larson and Wilford (1980) found that QOL is systematically related to per capita income. A.K. Sen warns against too narrow and too final a view of these results. Quality of life cannot be taken to be a substitute for income. Instead, he suggests calculating the expected life-time income (Gen, 1980:6). In our analysis, we take QOL along with other indicators of poverty separately.

In poverty analysis, it is useful to be concerned with results rather than inputs or supplies. The physical quality of life (QOL) index has the merit of measuring results rather than inputs.

Indicators of many conditions are used for constructing a measure of quality of life — individual status, technological development, individual equality, living conditions, economic status, agricultural production, educational development, etc. They consist of subjective and objective indicators. Such lists are never exhaustive enough to satisfy all uses, and they mix resources, causes and results. There is also the problem of *indicator overload.*

In this analysis, data permitting, it is attempted to keep close to QOL as defined by Morris. Confined to the 'end of process of development' measures, four indicators to define quality of life (4.1 to 4.4 in the next Section) are taken.

III
COMPLETE LIST OF INDICATORS OF POVERTY

A complete list of indicators used in this study to represent different aspects of poverty in regions of Indiz is given below.

I. Resource Deprivation and Resource Inequality.
II. Income Insufficiency and Income Inequality.
III. Nutritional Inadequacy

- 3.1 Ultra-poor poverty line; expenditure level needed to obtain 1920 calories per capita per day by rural person: UPPL
- 3.2 Poor poverty line; expenditure level necessary to obtain 2400 calories per capita per day: PPL
- 3.3 Percentage of ultra poor: PUP
- 3.4 Percentage of poor: PP

3.5 Percentage of expenditure on food items by households at ultra-poor poverty line: PEF. Alternatively, average per cent expenditure on food by households (AEF) is also tried.
3.6 Poverty-gap: PG
3.7 Disparity among the poor: DAP
3.8 Sen's index: SI

IV. Quality of Life: QOL since reliable data of birth and death do not exist at the district and regional level, recource will have to be had to proxies. The following indicators are chosen:

4.1 Percentage of rural households living in houses with 'Kutcha' walls (PRH)
4.2 Infant mortality rate (IMR)[13]
4.3 Survival ratio: Since the data about IMR and expectation of life are not complete and reliable, a proxy variable, survival ratio (SURR) is used. This is defined as the ratio of 1961 rural population surviving to 1971. This reflects the reverse of mortality. However, since the migratory streams have not been excluded from the population totals, the survival ratio reflects the effect of mortality as well as migration. Moreover, it does not help us in measuring infant mortality in any way.
4.4 Literacy rate among rural females (FLR)
Literacy is defined as the end result of the process of development leading to household welfare.

NOTES

1. There is widespread agreement that a person is in absolute poverty if and only if, and to the extent that his or her resources are too few to meet "basic needs by any combination of exchange and use" (Lipton, 1983:4).
2. The legitimacy of taking consumption expenditure as proxy to income is doubtful since income inequalities are normally greater than consumption inequalities (Planning Commission, 1978:3). Majority of poor households both in rural and urban areas dissave (Bhatty and Sarma, 1977:282-84).
3. Bhattacharya and associates have converted nominal average PCE into real average PCE across rural areas (1985 a) and urban areas (1985 b) of different states of India. For these they have computed regional price indices and interstate price differentials (Bhattacharya et al 1980, 1985 a,b) from NSS

consumption data pertaining to the 18th and 28th rounds (Chatterjee and Bhattacharya, 1974, Bhattacharya et al 1980).

4. All the above measures of poverty are unidimensional. What may be needed is a comprehensive measure. Dandekar (1981:1243) enumerates four criteria which may be used to define a poverty line. However, these criteria are used to determine an expenditure level which defines poverty line and not the chosen norm.
5. In at least one study, the Planning Commission (1981:7) calculated the percentage of people suffering from either calorie deficiency (<2300 calories) or protein deficiency (<57 gms) both in rural and urban areas in 1971-72 as 28.8 and 32.6 per cent respectively.
6. Also see Srinivasan (1979) it may be noted that the usual poverty measures are very sensitive to the precise nutritional norms chosen. Scandizzo and Knudsen (1979) have observed for Pakistan that varying nutritional norm from 90 per cent of the average requirement to 110 per cent increases the proportion of the malnourished from 0 per cent to 90 per cent (quoted by Srinivasan, 1979:14). It can be shown that acceptance of Sukhatme's suggestions will bias the estimates against the poor. Dandekar (1981:1250); Panda (1987); Das Gupta and Roy (1986) and Kakwani (1986). However, spatial differentials in poverty may or may not be sensitive to the norm chosen.
7. Others to use two poverty lines are Planning Commission (1981). NCAER (1986) and Panda (1987).
8. Sastry and Suryanarain (1981:97-117) take the proportion of the minimum monthly expenditure on non-food components to that on food components in rural areas to be 36 per cent.
9. See Sen (1983). Jain (1987), Kundu (1981:80-96) for the discussion of these axioms. Kakwani (1980) also suggested monotonicity sensitivity axiom and transfer sensitivity axiom I and II. In addition invariance and replication axioms are also suggested. They also examined different indicators in the light of these axioms.
10. The 14 measures of poverty used by Jain (1987) in his table numbers 5.2 to 5.7 have been put to correlation analysis. We report here the results of the exercise about rural poverty in 1960-61 for 15 states.

    All the composite indicators of poverty are highly correlated with each other. In most of the cases the coefficient of correlation is greater than 0.96. The simplest measure, i.e. the head-count ratio, is also uniformly highly correlated with all these compound and complex measures of poverty. In most cases the correlation coefficient is between 0.84 and 0.97.
11. Initially, J. Tinbergen and the Club of Rome suggested the computation of the quality of life index to be used in conjunction with per capital GNP. Larson and Wilford (1980) and Morris (1979) computed QOL index for 150 countries. Morris also computed the quality of life indicator for states in India. As already pointed out, Morris computed the indicator by assigning equal weights to life expectancy, infant mortality and literacy and found great divergence in this indicator and per capita GNP in most of the Indian States. Sen (1980), using similar concepts calculated excess expectation of life in comparison to per capita GNP.

12. The arbitrary selection of the included indicators and the arbitrariness in the choice of equal weight may render the physical quality of life indicator statistically unsound.
13. Bardhan (1984:201) finds that mortality, especially child mortality and more specifically female child mortality in rural India depends upon factors other than poverty in terms of household consumption or nutritional inadequacy. Hence infant mortality as a component of quality of life should be considered separately.

    Bardhan also finds that the survival chances of female child is related with employment and earning opportunities of female adults. He tests this hypothesis (Bardhan, 1982:210).

3

PRELIMINARY RESULTS ABOUT POVERTY IN INDIA : SENSITIVITY ANALYSIS

In this chapter, results based on the indicators listed in the preceding chapter are presented and sensitivity of poverty to the concept, norm and formula used in computing poverty is examined.

I
INTRODUCTION

As already pointed out, the household consumption expenditure data of the 27th round of NSS published in *Sarvekshana* (1983: S-1 to S-88) are used for calculating the nutritional inadequacy and income insufficiency indicators. The resource deprivation indicators have been computed from the All India Debt and Investment Survey, 1971-72 of R.B.I. Other dat; are processed from 1971 Census and other official publications.

Most of the researchers on poverty in India have adopted a monthly expenditure norm of Rs 15. at 1960-61 prices adjusted for price change over time and across regions/states. (Rao et al 1986:97; L.R. Jain et al 1988 : 2395; Mahendra Dev, 1986). Taking a uniform poverty-line expenditure for all periods and all regions cannot be defended since besides price variations other factors like regional differentials in dietary habits and temporal changes therein determine the expenditure required to attain the DER. Hence, we have computed the poverty line expenditure for each region separately on the basis of a uniform calorie norm for all regions. Following Lipton (1983 : 35-37), we compute two poverty lines — UPPL and PPL for each region separately

Linear interpolation between the two end-points of the

expenditure class containing the poverty line expenditure gives the per cent of population (households) under the poverty line. Information about 63 N.S.S. regions is processed in this way. Jammu and Kashmir (mountainous) calorie data distributed class-wise is not smooth and interpolation is impossible. This region has been left out of the study. The other nutrition based indicators have been derived from this basic source and the value of the poverty line ratio obtained above. The income insufficiency and inequality indicators have also been computed from the same source. However, data for the calculation of resource deprivation indicators have been obtained from RBI's All India Debt and Investment Survey, 1971-72. Other data have been derived from various sources, mainly from the census reports and Bardhan (1984).

In addition, percentage of household budget spent on food items is also calculated. In terms of Lipton's two-80 per cent criterion, the regions showing high ultra-poverty as well as a heavy budget allocation (exceeding 80 per cent) to food are considered to be in the most acute poverty situation.

Since there are two poverty lines there will be two variants of the indicators derived from them. Moreover, these can also be calculated with reference to the expenditure or calorie intake of different classes. These sets of indicators can be reduced and the problem of variable-overweight tackled by computing the first principal component of closely correlated indicators.

II
NUTRITIONAL INADEQUACY

The values of the means and C.V. of some of these indicators are given in Table 3.1. It is to be noted that the per capita household expenditure necessary to obtain 1920 calories (UPPL) as also to obtain 2400 calories (PPL) differs sharply among regions with mean of Rs. 32.09 (Rs. 47.67 for obtaining 2400 calories) and standard deviation of Rs. 8.19 (Rs. 12.23), the coefficient of variation being 25.5 per cent (25.6), testifying to quite high inter-regional differentials. However, these two measures are highly inter-correlated (r = 0.9467). Thus, classification of regions according to poverty line expenditure is not sensitive to the choice of the normative calorie requirement.

TABLE 3.1: Poverty-line and Percentage Poor: Correlation Matrix

n = 63

Index	UPPL	PPL	PUP	PP	PFE	AEF
UPPL	1					
PPL	0.9467*	1				
PUP	0.7187*	0.6379*	1			
PP	0.6901*	0.6907*	0.8902*	1		
PEF	−0.3715*	−0.3596*	−0.1393	0.0028	1	
AEF	0.1654	0.1401	0.3443*	0.4839*	0.6665*	1
MEAN	*32.09*	*47.76*	*34.78*	*62.83*	*79.87*	*72.34*
C.V.(%)	*25.51*	*25.61*	*61.25*	*36.33*	*5.08*	*7.31*

* Significant at one per cent level of significance

The percentage of ultra poor (PUP) is 34.8 and that of poor (including the ultra poor) is as high as 62.8. Thus, the incidence of poverty is highly sensitive to the calorie norms chosen. The inter-regional differentials in the percentage of poor is substantially higher in the case of the ultra poor (*C.V.* = 61.4) than the poor (including ultra poor) (*C.V.* = 36.3). There are thus vast regional differentials in nutritional inadequacy among 63 regions of India. However, the coefficient of correlation between the percentage poor (PP) and the percentage of ultra (PUP) is 0.8902. Though this relations is not as close as in the case of the poverty line expenditure, it is statistically highly significant. The distribution of regions in accordance with the percentage of population below poverty line is, thus, also not sensitive to the normative calorie requirements chosen.

A highly revealing result is that regions requiring higher per capita poverty line expenditure (PPL or UPPL) have also a higher proportion of persons under poverty line (r = 0.72 and 0.69). Table 3.1). Thus, if the poverty line expenditure can be reduced then the proportion of the poor will also get reduced. This can be done either by changing the consumption habits towards cheaper food or by changing the relative prices of the items of consumption. Another reason for the high poverty-line expenditure (UPPL, PPL) in some regions may be the relatively higher expenditure required for non-food items. This is supported by the statistically significant correlation of UPPL (and PPL) with the percentage of expenditure on food items by the ultra poor (PEF). However, the percentage of expenditure on food items of the ultra poor is not significantly correlated with the per cent poor or ultra poor. Thus, a high per cent of poor (or ultra poor) is found both among those who spend a higher proportion on food as among those who spend lower proportion. On an average, the ultra poor (i.e. those who are not able to obtain 1920 calories) spend 79.87 per cent of their total expenditure on food items and the standard deviation is also low at 4.0607, the coefficient of variation being 5.1. Hence, this indicator does not show much regional variations. In computing composite indicator of poverty, this indicator can perhaps be dropped.

Disparity Among the Poor (DAP)

It can be easily hypothesised that persons below poverty line, howsoever defined, are not equally poor. Hence, for policy purposes a measure of the distribution is also required. For this, it can be hypothesised that there are significant inter-regional differences in the distribution of the poor below the poverty line. We assume lognormality of the distribution of household expenditure among different expenditure classes. Standard deviation and Lorenz ratio of this distribution have been computed. In most of the cases the assumption of a two-parameter lognormal distribution hold in such studies. Hence, Lorenz ratio is calculated by fitting a two-parameter lognormal distribution to the households classified by per capita expenditure classes. Since the distributions of expenditure and calorie intake are different, the Lorenz ratio has been separately computed for these distributions. Thus, there are four Lorenz ratios, two for the ultra poor and two for the poor.

The average Lorenz ratio for the distribution of expenditure of the ultra poor comes to 0.1526 with standard deviation 0.0551. The same for the distribution of calories are 0.1239 and 0.0647, respectively. The average Lorenz ratios based on expenditure and calories for the poor are 0.1799 and 0.1266 with standard deviation .0526 and .0491, respectively. Thus, there are very high inter-regional differentials exhibited by the Lorenz ratios in accordance with all the four measures. The coefficient of variation ranges between 29.2 per cent and 52.2 per cent. However, the correlation between these four measures, though positive and high (range 0.45 to 0.85) is far from perfect. Thus, distributions according to expenditure and calories differ substantially. Hence, a composite indicator of disparity among the poor has been computed using the principal component analysis. Only the first principal component is calculated since it explains as high as 73.61 per cent of the total variance in the four indicators. The relative weights assigned are 0.2519, 0.2343, 0.2533 and 0.2605. The weights derived from the principal component method have been applied to the standardised variates to derive a standardised composite indicator of disparities among the poor (DAP).

Since there are vast disparities in the distribution of expenditure and calories among the poor, the head-count measure cannot be sufficient for policy decisions. It should be supplemented with a measure of disparities.

Poverty Gap (PG)

As already explained, poverty gap measures the extent to which the total expenditure of the poor should be increased in order to pull up the poor to the poverty level. Four measures of poverty gap, two for the poor and two for the ultra poor related to expenditure-gap and calorie-gap, have been computed. The expenditure and calorie gaps for the ultra poor are, on an average, equal to 23.39 and 20.40 per cent, and the coefficient of variation equal to 30.39 and 43.3, respectively. This implies that, on an average, the ultra poor household's per capita expenditure and calorie intake are 23.39 and 20.40 per cent below the poverty line expenditure and normative calorie intake. The same for the poor are 30 and 23.1 per cent, respectively. The substantial values of CVs reveal that expenditure gap and calorie gap give different estimates of the dimensions of the problem of poverty. The distributions of regions in accordance with the four measures are also not exactly similar, as revealed by the relatively low zero-order correlations. Since there is nothing to choose between the four, a composite indicator of poverty gap, based on these four measures, has been computed. The first principal component explains 67.26 per cent of the variance in the four indicators. The relative weights are : 0.2989, 0.2225, 0.1875, and 0.2910.

Sen's Index (SI)

Sen's index is a composite indicator of poverty gap, head-count ratio and Lorenz ratio. As in other cases, four indicators using Sen's formula have been computed. These are based on the distribution of expenditure and calorie for the ultra poor and the poor. The average values of Sen's index for the ultra poor are 0.1781 and 0.1425 and for the poor 0.3764 and 0.2789, respectively. There are very large inter-regional differentials in the value of Sen's index by all these measures as revealed by the CV which ranges between 47.3 to 77.6 per cent. However, as revealed by the zero-order correlation coefficients between these four indicators, these are very highly inter-correlated. Sen's index for the poor exhibits uniformly high correlations with all the other three indicators. Therefore, this would represent the poverty measure based on Sen's index.

2. Income Insufficiency

Average Per Capita Household Expenditure (APE)

The per capita expenditure of all households is often taken as a proxy of per capita income as well as the relative level of development of the region. In general, it can be shown that, if prices are the same in all the regions, the higher the per capita expenditure the lower will be poverty, given that the distribution of households by per capita expenditure does not vary between regions. Thus, high per capita expenditure does not imply low poverty in all situations. The average per capita expenditure of all regions is 46.63 with the standard deviation equal to 10.6932; thus, the coefficient of variation is 22.93 per cent.

Since the relative prices in different regions are different, for inter-regional comparison, the per capita real expenditure (RY) should be taken. It is seen that the poverty line expenditure varies from region to region. This may be because of variations in diets and relative prices as well as in the expenditure on non-food items. The expenditure on non-food items is not highly correlated with poverty expenditure. Moreover, it does not show significant inter-regional differentials. Hence, the hypothesis that regions with high per capita expenditure should show low percentage of expenditure on food items (i.e negative correlation) is not supported by the data presented here, though r is negative (= -.38) but it is not significant at 5 per cent level. Thus, the differences in the poverty line expenditure are mainly because of the first two factors, i.e. differences in diet and relative prices. Therefore, in order to calculate the per capita real expenditure, the per capita nominal expenditure (i.e. APE) has been divided by per capita poverty line expenditure (UPPL). This gives the per capita real expenditure in terms of the standardised calorie norm (RY). Values greater than one would indicate that the average expenditure in the region can provide the normative diet and related expenditure to more than one person. The higher the value of this real expenditure the higher is the standard above the poverty line expenditure. In order that this reflects poverty and not standard of living, the signs of the standardised scores will have to be changed.

The average real expenditure index comes to 1.5532 and the coefficient of variation 37.8 per cent. It may be noted that though the variances in nominal expenditure and poverty-line expenditure (UPPL) are quite low (Table 3.1) the variance in real expenditure is quite high.

Inequality in the Distribution of Income (Expenditure)

Other things remaining the same, the percentage under poverty-line would be large if the disparity among the households is large. Hence, computation of the index of disparity would be useful. Two sets of indicators are used, one based on the Lorenz ratio and the other on the crude indicators of concentration defined on median and quartiles (m, m', m_1) as follows:[1]

$$m = \frac{(100\text{-}M)}{M}; m^1 = \frac{(100\text{-}Q_3)}{Q_1}; = m_1 \frac{M\text{-}Q_1}{Q_1}$$

where, M, Q_1 and Q_3 are the median first and third quartiles, respectively the m_1 measures intra-poor inequalities. m (m') gives the ratio of assets held by to the top 50 per cent (top 25 per cent) to those held by the bottom 50 per cent (bottom 25 per cent) households.

The Lorenz ratios of distribution of expenditure (LY_1) and calories (LY_2) are not the same (r=.58). Hence, a composite indicator has been calculated, which explains 79.0 per cent of variance in LY_1 and LY_2. The average Lorenz ratio of distribution of households by expenditure classes is .2514 with CV equal to 18.7 per cent. The standard deviation of the Lorenz ratios and concentration ratios are quite low in comparison to the mean values, so that regional variations in the concentration pattern are not very large (CV ranges from 9.5 to 21.9 per cent). The median-based concentration ratio is 2.18 and the quartile based ratio is 3.46.

It follows that the top 50 per cent households have cornered 2.18 times the income of the bottom 50 per cent and the top 25 per cent 3.46 times of the bottom 25 per cent rural households. Among the bottom half, the disparities are not so high, m_1 being as low as 1.48. It is to be noted that m and m' which are based on the median and quartile, respectively, are highly intercorrelated (r=0.95). The composite indicator of concentration of income explains 77.6 per cent of the variance in the three indicators. As revealed by the CV (ranging between 7.5 and 21.9 per cent), the regional variation in disparity ratio is relatively low.

3. Resource Deprivation

As already pointed out, deprivation in terms of availability and distribution of land, assets and employment has been considered. The following variables are initially included. They all relate to 1971.

1. Percentage of households having assets less than Rs. 2500 ($PLAHH)_1$).
2. Percentage of households having assets less than Rs. 5000 ($PLAHH_2$).
3. Percentage of households owning land less than 2.5 acres ($PLLHH_1$).
4. Percentage of households owning land less than 5.0 acres ($PLLHH_2$).
5. Concentration of assets with the top 25 per cent asset holders in comparison to the bottom 25 per cent asset holders (CA).
6. Concentration of value of land owned (CVLO).
7. Rural unemployment rate (URR) — Average daily rural unemployment rate in the region.
8. Average land owned (ALO) or Pressure on land (POL).

Variables 1 and 7 have been computed from All India Rural Debt and Investment Survey 1971-72 of RBI. Variable 8 (URR) has been taken from Pranab Bardhan (1984, Appendix Table C: 288-230.).

On an average, 32.34 and 48.52 per cent of rural households own assets less than Rs. 2500 and Rs. 5000, respectively (Table 3.2).

However, as high as 58.19 and 74.47 per cent of the rural households own land less than 2.5 and 5.0 acres. The regional variations in the distribution of assets (*CV*=40.4) is larger than in the distribution of land (*CV*=28.8). Similarly, the concentration of assets shows very large inter-regional variations, *CV* being as high as 70.2. On an average, the top 25 per cent of the households have 46 times the value of assets with the bottom 25 per cent households. Since the pattern is regionally highly differentiated, this ought to have significant impact on the other poverty measures. It is revealing to note that it is much higher than the concentration ratio of income. Thus, resource inequalities are much more acute than the expenditure disparities. On an average, land owned is equal to 4.57 acres, and it is expected that larger value of average land owned should be negatively correlated with indicators of poverty. This assumption is supported by data (Table 3.2). Hence, it would be better to calculate an indicator which is reciprocal of this indicator. In fact, an index of pressure on land defined as the number of households per 100 acres of land has been calculated.

POL = 100/average land owned

The correlation matrix (Table 3.2) reveals that variables $PLAHH_1$. and $PLAHH_2$ are highly intercorrelated (r=0.93). Similarly, variables $PLLHH_1$ and $PLLHH_2$ are highly mutually correlated (r=0.91). But other variables do not show high intercorrelation. In particular, the unemployment rate which, though positively correlated with the land and asset disparity indicators, does not show high values of the coefficient of correlation. However, unemployment rate at 7.37 per cent shows high inter-regional differentials (coefficient of variation is as high as 74.7 per cent). A composite indicators from the set of some of these indicators has, therefore, been computed. The final set of variables depicting resource deprivation is as follows:

1. Asset deprivation (AD) consisting of variable PLAHH.
2. Land deprivation (LD) consisting of variable $PLAHH_1$ and the indicator of pressure on land (POL)
3. Concentration of assets and land (COLA).
4. Unemployment rate (URR).

TABLE 3.2: **Resource Deprivation : Correlation Matrix**

	$PLAHH_1$	$PLAHH_2$	$PLLHH_1$	$PLLHH_2$	CA	CVLO	URR	ALO
1. $PLAHH_1$	1							
2. $PLAHH_2$	.93	1						
3. $PLLHH_1$	.49	.44	1					
4. $PLLHH_2$	.34	.36	.91	1				
5. CA	.64	.46	.34	.13	1			
6. CVLO	.5	.42	.57	.35	.62	1		
7. URR	.43	.38	.49	.35	.23	.36	1	
8. ALO	−.33	−.35	−.85	−.96	−.15	−.36	−.30	1
MEAN	*32.3*	*48.5*	*58.2*	*74.5*	*45.9*	*146.4*	*7.4*	*4.6*
C.V.(%)	*40.4*	*29.0*	*28.8*	*21.8*	*70.2*	*27.8*	*74.0*	*67.0*

4. Quality of Life

The physical quality of life measures the end result of the process of socio-economic development and social welfare policies of the state. As already pointed out three indicators representing quality of life or lack of it have been taken here:

SURR = Survival ratio (1961-1971) as a proxy for expectation of life.
FLR = Literacy rate among rural female. 100-LR gives the female illiteracy rate.
PKH = Per cent of Kutcha houses in total rural houses.

The zero-order correlation matrix and the important ratios are given in Table 3.3.

The inter-region variance in SURR is low but that in literacy and per cent of Kutcha houses is quite large. However, it ought to be noted that the three variables are not significantly correlated with each other, hence a composite indicator of quality of life cannot be constructed. The variables will have to be taken up separately.

TABLE 3.3: Quality of Life: Zero-Order Correlations

	SURR	FLR	PKH
SURR	1		
FLR	.02	1	
PKH	−.13	−.05	1
MEAN	.8827	13.49	55.05
CV	13.52	71.76	39.87

A priori, quality of life is expected to be high in regions exhibiting low nutritional poverty. The signs of regression (as well as correlation) coefficients of poverty with survival ratio and literacy rate are expected to be negative and that with per cent of kutcha houses positive. However, the hypotheses stand verified only in the case of survival ratio. Regressing PUP and APE on the quality of life indicator, the following results are obtained (Table 3.4).

TABLE 3.4: Poverty and Quality of Life Indicators : Regression Results

Explanatory variables	Dependent variables			
	PUP		APE	
	β	t	β	t
SURR	−.1695*	−2.1857	1.7110	.1443
FLR	1.0050	4.8431	.0708	.4876
PKH	-8.9×10^{-4}*	−1.9293	.1183	1.8328

R^2 = .3687. F = 10.5123

The higher the survival ratio (the lower the mortality rate), the lower is poverty. This result is usually hypothesised. However, poverty is low in regions with relatively higher female illiteracy. Though the result is shocking and difficult to explain, it is not novel. Similar results were obtained by other scholars (Jain, 1987; Rao et al 1986 : 98). Similar remarks hold for the unexpected negative sign of the coefficient of PKH.

One common reason of such results is errors in model specification. All these variables are themselves endogenous variables. In fact, they depend much more on poverty, income and resources than the other way round. Moreover, achievements in the field of quality of life indicated by, to modify Sen's phrase, excess quality of life, depend more on social welfare policies, work of non-government voluntary agencies, historical coincidences, natural conditions and social and cultural practices and institutions than on purely economic magnitudes.

III
SENSITIVITY OF POVERTY MEASURE

There are, thus, a number of criteria and norms for defining and measuring poverty and a host of formulae, each having its own merits and limitations. It is, therefore, necessary to test the sensitivity of poverty measurement to the choice of norm and formula.

It has already been shown (Table 3.1) that the proportion of households under poverty line jumps up from 34.78 to 62.83 per cent when the energy norm is changed from 1920 and 2400 calories. However, the same Table 3.1 reveals that inter-regional differentials are not sensitive to this choice. The zero-order coefficients of correlation between the different indicators (Table 3.5) show that the nutritional indicators PUP, PG and SI are highly and positively intercorrelated. These can easily be combined into a composite indicator of nutritional inadequacy. The income insufficiency indicator in real terms is also highly correlated with the nutritional poverty indicators. However, the indicators of income inequalities among the poor as well as all rural households are not so highly related to the nutritional poverty indicators. So is the case of the various resource deprivation indicators, including the unemployment rate, though the signs of the relationships are as expected. The quality-of-life indicators give an altogether different picture of poverty as compared to all the other indicators. Hence, there is need for considering different poverty indicators separately for representing different aspects of the problem.

TABLE 3.5: Correlation between Different Indicators of Poverty

Indicator	PUP	PG	SI	RY	DAP	LY	AD	LD	COLA	UR
PUP	1									
PG	.88*	1								
SI	.94*	.90*	1							
RY	.88*	.73*	.86*	1						
DAP	.47*	.68*	.61*	.25*	1					
LY	.48*	.62*	.52*	.31*	.57*	1				
AD	.60*	.61*	.68*	.59*	.47*	.34*	1			
LD	.33*	.46*	.43*	.29*	.36*	.21*	.45	1		
COLA	.31*	.44*	.37*	.29*	.44*	.28*	.65*	.43*	1	
URR	.57*	.61*	.59*	.46*	.50*	.31*	.46*	.51*	.24*	1

Note: COLA = Composite indicator of CA, CVOL and POL

IV
CONCLUSIONS

These preliminary results show that poverty is widespread and there are vast regional differentials. Though the indicators of nutritional inadequacy and income insufficiency are closely related, the relationship is far from perfect. The indicators of concentration of income and resources as well as quality of life tell a story different from what the positional indicators reveal. Hence, different indicators have to be used to represent poverty in the regions of India. Taking solely nutrition based poverty indicator/indicators as the criterion for policy-making decisions regarding distribution of physical and financial resources and other developmental issues cannot be justified.

In this scheme, regions with a low asset base, high resource inequality, high unemployment rate, low income and high income inequality, high nutritional inadequacy despite the allotment of a high proportion of household budget to food, and low quality of life are the worst cases of poverty. However, different combinations of these conditions are possible. They would pose different problems and present different prospects.

It is thus clear that the poverty profile of each region ought to be prepared taking into account most of these indicators. This will help in designing region specific poverty alleviation programmes.

These results also show convincingly that regional differences in poverty are not sensitive with respect of the nutritional norm chosen or the particular formula used to calculate the nutrition based indicator of poverty. However, whatever norm and index may be used to compute the food inadequacy-based measure of poverty, there is no one-to-one correspondence between the pattern revealed by this index and the other measures considered here, namely, resources deprivation, unemployment, income insufficiency, income and resource inequality and quality of life. Hence, the debate about the nutrition norm and axiomatic properties of different indicators should not be permitted to divert attention from the highly complex problem of understanding poverty. In fact, the regional poverty scenario is not only very complicated but, structurally, it is highly differentiated too.

NOTE

1. James Naya and Meier (1988 : 201-203) use a similar indicator based on quintiles. See also Oshima (1988 : Ch.8).

4

RURAL POVERTY PROFILES OF THE REGIONS ON THE BASIS OF POVERTY INDICATORS

I
INTRODUCTION

Usually poverty studies are undertaken with respect to a calorie norm. However, a strong case can be made for considering poverty in terms of the proximate inputs (like income) or ultimate inputs (physical and human capital resources) or the end results of the use of resources (quality of life). In our study, we define and measure poverty in terms of all these four aspects. In all the above four cases poverty may be defined in absolute or relative terms. Again, after deciding about the definition of poverty, the problem of developing a suitable indicator has also to be faced.

In this chapter, the following sets of poverty indicators are used.

I. *Nutritional Inadequacy* (*1972-73*)

1.	PUP	Percentage ultrapoor (Head-count ratio, H)
2.	PP	Percentage poor
3.	PG	Poverty Gap
4.	SI	Sen's Index
5.	PEF	Percentage outlay on food at ultrapoor poverty line
6.	APE	Average per capita expenditure (in Rs.)
7.	RY	Real Income (= APE/UPPL)
8.	LY	Composite index of inequality in the distribution of expenditure
9.	AVA	Average value of total assets held by rural household on 1st June 1971

10.	AD	Asset deprivation
11.	LD	Percentage of households owning land less than 2.5 acres. Index of land deprivation ($PLLHH_1$)
12.	COLA	Composite lines of concentration of land and assets
13.	URR	Rural Unemployment rate
14.	FILLR	Female illiteracy rate
15.	SURR	Survival ratio
16.	PKH	Percentage of Kutcha Houses (Rural)
17.	DAP	Composite indicator of expenditure/calorie inequality among the poor

The indicators of nutritional inadequacy, income insufficiency, resource deprivation and quality of life of 63 NSS regions are processed here. Every variable is standardised and the standardised (Z) scores are classified into seven groups. The group at about the Indian average (A) is expected to contain approximately 30 per cent of the districts (about 19 districts). The above and below average[1] categories consist of 35 per cent of districts each, subdivided into very very high, very high and high sub-categories on the above average (high) side. In terms of the usual poverty measures they will have high to very high poverty. Similar subdivision is done on the below average (low) side.

Z-Score	*Poverty category*
−1.6450 to −∝	Very Very Low (VVL)
−1.0365 to −1.6450	Very Low (VL)
−0.3854 to −1.0365	Low (L)
−0.3854 to 0.3854	Average (A)
0.3854 to 1.0365	High (H)
1.0365 to 1.6450	Very High (VH)
1.6450 to ∝	Very Very High (VVH)

After describing the performance of the regions in accordance with the various poverty indicators, the regions are clustered into groups with respect to these indicators.

II
DISTRIBUTION OF REGIONS BY POVERTY MEASURES

Nutritional Inadequacy

Distributions of regions by ultrapoverty and poverty are nearly normal. On an average 62.8 and 34.8 per cent of rural households are under poverty and ultrapoverty lines respectively. Twenty-three regions have high to very high ultrapoverty; twenty-eight regions are in this category with respect to poverty norm of 2400 calories (Table 4.1a, col. 1 and 3). There is no region with very low ultrapoverty, though there are six regions in this category according to the poverty norm. As already reported, there is very high correlation between the proportion of the poor and ultrapoor. Since we have adopted the two — 80 per cent criterion for poverty analysis, we shall drop the percentage under poverty line from our list of the measures of poverty and consider only the percentage under ultrapoverty line as the head-count ratio.

The other variable, per cent expenditure on food at the ultrapoverty line, is also approximately distributed as a normal variate. In ten regions, the per cent outlay on food at the ultrapoverty line is much higher than 80 per cent (Table 4.1a, col. 5, 6). Of these, region 9 (Eastern, Gujarat) has very high ultrapoverty. Thus, in this region, very large number of people are not able to get even 80 per cent of DER despite spending much more than 80 per cent of their budget on food. Similarly, Southern Bihar (6), Southern Orissa (37), Southern Rajasthan (43), West Bengal Plains (57) and Eastern Plains (55) have very high poverty despite much above average spending on food. However, Inland Eastern M.P. (22), Northern M.P. (25), Western Rajasthan (41), Tripura (48), Eastern U.P. (52), Manipur Plains (58) and Hills (59) have achieved below average poverty because of relatively heavier spending on food items, thus, neglecting other requirements. This must have adverse consequences for quality of life.

In contrast, Kerala (19, 20), Inland Western Maharashtra (27) and Coastal Northern Maharashtra (26) have very high poverty, and Southern Gujarat Plains (11), Inland Northern A.P. (2), Southern Bihar (6), Inland Eastern Maharashtra (30), Eastern Maharashtra (31) and Inland Northern Maharashtra (28) exhibit high poverty but relatively very low or low expenditure on food. Thus their malnutrition is caused by factors other than insufficient spending capacity. Poverty situation in these can be alleviated to some extent by judicious budget planning (Table 4.1a, col. 2 and 6).

Eastern Haryana (14), H.P. (16), Inland Southern Karnataka (34), Northern Punjab (39), Meghalaya (60) and Delhi (61) are the best regions as they have low poverty achieved by spending less than

TABLE 4.1a: Nutritional Inadequacy: Distribution of Regions

Sl. No. Indicators/ Categories	Percentage Ultra Poor (PUP)		Percentage Poor (PP)		Percentage Outlay on Food at Poverty Line (PEF)		Disparity Among the Poor (DAP)		Poverty Gap (PG)		Sen's Index (SI)	
	Serial No. of Regions	f	Serial No. of Regions	f	Serial No. of Regions	f	Serial No. of Regions	f	Serial No. of Regions	f	Serial No. of Regions	f
	1	2	3	4	5	6	7	8	9	10	11	12
(1) Very Very Low (VVL)	—	—	14, 15, 18, 25, 39, 40	6	11, 20, 39, 61, 63	5	—	—	—	—	18, 39, 14	3
(2) Very Low (VL)	14, 15, 16, 17, 18, 25, 39, 40, 41, 53, 61	11	16, 42, 44, 53, 61	5	19, 27, 33, 45, 60	5	14, 16, 17, 40, 42, 53, 58, 59	8	14, 17, 18, 40, 53, 58, 59	7	15, 16, 17, 25, 40, 41, 42, 44, 53, 59	10
(3) Low (L)	22, 34, 42, 44, 48, 50, 51, 52, 58, 59, 60, 24	12	17, 41, 48, 50, 51, 52	6	5, 14, 16, 26, 28, 30, 31, 34, 47	9	4, 5, 10, 12, 13, 15, 22, 41, 44, 46, 48, 49, 50, 51, 52, 60	16	5, 10, 15, 16, 22, 23, 25, 41, 42, 44, 50, 51, 52, 60, 61	15	10, 13, 22, 34, 48, 50, 51, 52, 58, 60	10

(4) Average (A)	2, 3, 4, 5, 7, 8, 10, 12, 13, 21, 23, 29, 33, 35, 36, 47, 49, 63	18	2, 3. 7, 8, 10, 11, 21, 22. 23, 24, 33, 34, 35, 36, 47, 49, 58, 59	19	1, 3, 4, 15, 17, 18, 23, 24, 29, 36, 38, 40, 42, 44, 46, 50, 51, 53, 54, 56, 62	21	1, 2, 7, 8, 9, 11, 18, 21, 23, 24, 25, 27, 30, 31, 32, 34, 37, 43, 47, 54, 62	21	1, 2, 4, 7, 8, 12, 13, 21, 24, 34, 36, 39, 43, 46, 48, 49, 54, 62, 63	19	2, 4, 5, 8, 12, 21, 23, 24, 46, 49, 61	11
(5) HIgh (H)	1, 6, 11, 28, 32, 37, 43, 46, 54, 55, 56, 57, 62	13	1, 4, 5, 6, 9, 12, 13, 28, 29, 30, 32, 37, 38, 43, 46, 54, 55, 56, 57, 63, 60	21	2, 6, 7, 8, 12, 13, 35, 37, 48, 52, 57, 58, 32	13	36, 20, 33, 35, 36, 45, 55, 57	11	3, 6, 9, 26, 27, 28, 29, 30, 31, 32, 33, 35, 37, 45, 47	15	1, 3, 9, 11, 27, 29, 30, 31, 32, 33, 35, 36, 37, 43, 47, 54, 62, 63, 67	20
(6) Very High (VH)	9, 26, 27, 30, 31, 38, 45	7	19, 20, 26, 27, 31, 45, 62	7	9, 10, 21, 22, 25, 43, 55, 59	8	19, 26, 38, 39 56	5	11, 38, 55, 56, 57	5	26, 28, 45, 55, 56, 57	6
(7) Very-Very High (VVH)	19, 20	2	—	—	41, 49	2	29, 61	2	19, 20	2	19, 20, 38	3
Missing/Total	64	63	64	63	64	63	64	63	64	63	64	63

80 per cent of the budget on food items. This can be supposed to arise because of higher nominal or real income/total expenditure per capita. In fact, region 14, 16, 39 and 61 have much above average per capita expenditure and region 14, 39 and 61 much above per capita real income than the all India average. However, Inland Southern Karnataka (34) and Meghalaya (60) are relatively poor or average from the point of view of nominal or real income and still they have achieved low poverty with below average proportion of expenditure on food items (Table 4.1b).

Thus, the achievers, those with low poverty, can be divided into three groups: (i) those who are able to do so because of high to very high budget allocation to food items (seven regions), (ii) those who allocate approximately 80 per cent of the budget to food (nine regions) and (iii) those who allocate low proportion but still achieve the DER, may be the price factor favours them (six regions).

TABLE 4.1b: Distribution of Regions according to Poverty and Percentage Expenditure on Food (PEF)

Poverty	Percentage Expenditure on Food			Total
	High (H, VH, VVH)	Average	Low (L, VL, VVL)	
High	9 6, 32, 37, 43, 55 57 (7)	38 1, 46, 54, 56 62, 24 (7)	19, 20 26, 27, 45, 30 11, 28, 31 (9)	23
Average	2, 7, 8, 35, 12 10, 21, 49, 13 (9)	3, 4 23, 29, 36 (5)	33, 47, 63 5 (4)	18
Low	25, 41 48, 52, 59, 58 22 (7)	15, 17, 18 40, 53, 42 44, 50, 51 (9)	14, 16, 39, 61 34, 60 (6)	22
Total	23	21	19	63

Similarly, the laggards can also be categorised into three groups: (i) those who are unable to achieve DER despite spending much more than 80 per cent of the budget on food items (7 regions), (ii) those who are poor despite spending nearly 80 per cent on food items, and lastly (iii) those who cannot achieve the DER because of quite low allocation to food for one reason or the other (9 regions) (Table 4.1b). The poverty situation in the first two groups is really very critical.

Of the eighteen regions having all India average poverty proportion, nine allocate much more than 80 per cent to food items, five about 80 per cent and only four below 80 per cent. Thus, besides the twenty three regions in high to very very high poverty categories, nine in the average poverty category are also the areas of acute problem on the basis of the two-80 per cent criterion.

Income Insufficiency

Nominal and Real Expenditure (Income)

All the nine very very high and very high nutritionally deficient regions are also high real income deficient. Excepting regions 20 and 27, this is also true of nominal expenditure (Table 4.2, col. 2 and 4). Hence, low income is one of the proximate causes of acute poverty in these regions. Of the remaining fourteen high poverty regions, except region 24, all have below average real income level. Hence, poverty stricken regions are low income areas.

Of the twenty-three relatively poorer regions, thirteen regions also have concentration of income in favour of the relatively affluent households. Only regions 27, 46 and 62 have below average concentration of income (Table 4.2, col. 6 and 8). However, all the three have very low levels of per capita real income. In most of the cases low income and highly unequal distribution of income reinforce each other and cause high levels of poverty.

Poverty Gap and Sen's Index

The distributions of regions by poverty gap and Sen's index are nearly normal. All the 9 regions in the very high and very very high poverty categories have very high poverty gap and Sen's index. Similar remarks hold for regions in high poverty category. Thus, the Head-count ratio can represent the poverty profiles based on the other nutrition based indicators very well.

Fortunately, of the 9 regions with very high poverty only three have much above average intra-poor disparities in the distribution of average per capita expenditure (DAP). These regions are: 19, 26 and

TABLE 4.2: Distribution of Regions by Income Insufficiency

Sl. No.	Indicators/ Categories	Per Capita Expenditure (APE)		Real Expenditure (RY)		Concentration of Expenditure (CY)		Lorenz Ratio (LR)	
		Serial No. of Regions	f	Serial No. of Regions	f	Serial No. of Regions	f	Serial No. of Regions	f
		1	2	3	4	5	6	7	8
(1)	Very-Very Low (VVL)	11, 14, 15, 16, 39, 40, 61	7	14, 18, 25, 39, 40, 61	6	4, 60	2	40, 58, 60, 17	4
(2)	Very Low (VL)		0	15, 42, 53	3	5, 13, 17, 18, 46, 58, 59	7	4, 5, 42	3
(3)	Low (L)	18, 25, 41, 42, 58, 60	6	16, 17, 23, 41, 44, 50, 51	7	12, 31, 48, 49, 52, 53, 54, 62	8	12, 13, 22, 27, 46, 48, 49, 52, 53, 59, 62	11

(4)	Average (A)	3, 8, 12, 13, 20, 23, 24, 27, 29, 31, 32, 33, 34, 36, 44, 48, 49, 50, 51, 52, 53, 59, 62, 63	24	3, 7, 8, 10, 12, 21, 22, 24, 29, 34, 36, 47, 48, 49, 52, 58, 59, 63	18	1, 2, 7, 9, 10, 14, 15, 16, 19, 22, 26, 27, 28, 32, 34, 37, 41, 43, 45, 50, 51, 63	22	1, 2, 9, 10, 14, 15, 16, 18, 21, 25, 28, 31, 32, 34, 37, 39, 41, 44, 47, 50, 51, 59, 61, 63	24
(5)	High (H)	1, 2, 4, 5, 6, 7, 9, 10, 17, 19, 26, 28, 30, 35, 45, 46, 47, 56, 57	20	1, 2, 4, 5, 6, 9, 11, 13, 26, 28, 30, 31, 32, 33, 35, 37, 38, 43, 45, 46, 54, 55, 56, 57, 60, 62	26	3, 6, 8, 20, 21, 23, 24, 30, 33, 35, 36, 38, 39, 42, 44, 47, 57, 61	18	3, 6, 7, 8, 19, 20, 26, 29, 30, 35, 36, 45, 23, 24	14
(6)	Very High (VH)	21, 22, 38, 43, 55	5	19, 20, 27	3	11, 25, 29, 40, 56	5	11, 38, 55, 56, 57, 33	6
(7)	Very-Very High (VVH)	37	1	—	—	55	1	43	1
	Missing/Total	64	63	64	63	64	63	64	63

38. In region 20 also the disparities among the poor are high but not too high. Similar remarks hold good about regions 6, 28, 55, 56 and 57 in the high poverty category. DAP is low in other regions (Table 4.1a, col. 8). Thus, high poverty is not caused by intra-poor maldistribution but because of overall inequalities in the distribution of income and assets.

Resource Deprivation

Three, six and twelve regions have very very high, very high and high land deprivation in relation to all India average. There is no region in the very very low category. In the other two categories there are nine and fourteen regions (Table 4.3, col. 4). Distributions of regions by land and asset deprivation are more or less symmetrical and normal. Regions 19, 20, 56, 1, 36, 45, 46, 47 and 49 have very high land deprivation and regions 1, 37, 45, 46, 11, 32, 47, 54, 55 and 56 very high asset deprivation.

Of the 9 regions in the very very high and very high nutritional poverty categories, three — Kerala (19, 20) and Coastal Northern Tamilnadu (45) — have very high land deprivation of the poor and four i.e., Eastern Plains Gujarat (9), Inland Western Maharashtra (27), Inland Eastern (30) and Eastern Maharashtra (31) have relatively very low land deprivation. However, among the fourteen regions with high poverty, the deprivation of the poor of the all important asset, land, is very severe in as many as seven regions (1, 11, 32, 46, 54, 55, 56 and 57); only in regions 24, 28, 43 and 64 is deprivation relatively low. Redistribution of land in favour of the very poor may help in these land deprived poverty-stricken regions.

Of the eleven very low poverty regions, three regions — region number 18, 39 and 61 have land deprivation of the poor on the higher side, all the other have low or very low land deprivation. Thus, land deprivation of the poor causes poverty, however, this alone cannot explain the phenomenon fully.

There are ten regions of acute asset deprivation of the poor and twelve of above average asset deprivation (Table 4.3, col. 2). The land and asset deprivation profiles do not fully tally with each other, so also the concentration of assets and land (COLA) profiles. Thus, to some extent, they capture different aspects of resource deprivation. Of the twelve regions with acute asset deprivation only five (regions 1, 45, 46, 47 and 56) also have acute land deprivation and only four (regions 1, 11, 46 and 47) have acute concentration of land and assets (Table 4.3).

Of the nine acute poverty ridden regions, only region 45 (Coastal Northern Tamilnadu) has a very very high asset deprivation and regions 19, 26, 30, 38 have high asset deprivation. Similarly, only regions 20, 30 and 45 have high concentration of assets and land. Region 31 (Eastern Maharashtra) with very high poverty has both low asset and land deprivation. Expectedly, in this region real income is low.

Though unemployment rate is low in India as a whole, there are wide inter-regional variations. A relatively high unemployment rate in rural areas implies that households with meagre or no productive assets are doubly handicapped. Even though the unemployment rate is low as compared to the proportion under the poverty line, howsoever, defined and measured, a relatively high unemployment rate does indicate a labour surplus rural labour market. If geographical mobility within the region is not restricted then this also implies a labour surplus overall regional labour market. Hence, rural wages and incomes are likely to be depressed resulting in higher poverty. Even if the overall correlation in not high, simultaneous cases of income insufficiency, nutritional inadequacy and unemployment are to be expected.

Distribution of regions by unemployment rate is not normal. It is skewed and platykurtic; the number of regions with average URR is relatively small. In all, twenty-seven regions have below average and eighteen above average unemployment. Regions 19, 20, 54, 18, 28, 31, 45, 46 and 57 exhibit very high unemployment rates. In contrast, regions 5, 16, 17, 43, 44, 49 and 64 have very low unemployment rates.

Of the nine acute nutritionally deficient regions, regions 19, 20, 31 and 45 have much above average unemployment rate, regions 30 and 38 also have high unemployment rates. On the other side of the picture, of the eleven regions of very low nutritional inadequacy, all except two regions (16 and 39) have relatively low (below average) unemployment rates. Of the remaining fourteen regions with high poverty, regions 1, 28, 46, 54, 55 and 57 have high to very high unemployment.

Region 43 (Southern Rajasthan) is an exception, it has very high poverty but unemployment is very low. Hence, productivity must be at a very low level. This is supported by the fact that nominal expenditure and real income per capita are very low in this region.

TABLE 4.3: Distribution of Regions by Resource Deprivation

Sl. No.	Indicators/ Categories	Asset Deprivation (AP)		Land Deprivation (LD)		Concentration of Asset & Land (COLA)		Unemployment Rate (URR)	
		Serial No. of Regions	f	Serial No. of Regions	f	Serial No. of Regions	f	Serial No. of Regions	f
		1	2	3	4	5	6	7	8
(1)	Very-Very Low (VVL)	16, 17, 18, 64	4	–	–	–	–	–	–
(2)	Very Low (VL)	15, 42, 44	3	12, 23, 24, 25, 29, 35, 41, 42, 44	9	4, 5, 17, 18, 41, 43, 51, 64	8	5, 16, 17, 43, 44, 49, 64	7
(3)	Low (L)	5, 10, 12, 14, 24, 25, 31, 39, 40, 41, 43, 49, 50, 52, 61	5	5, 9, 13, 15, 21, 22, 27, 28, 30, 31, 40, 43, 53, 64	14	6, 12, 22, 24, 25, 42, 44, 48, 50, 53, 54	11	4, 10, 11, 13, 14, 15, 21, 22, 23, 25, 32, 37, 40, 41, 42, 50, 51, 52, 53, 61	20

(4)	Average (A)	4, 6, 8, 9, 13, 20, 21, 22, 23, 27, 29, 35, 51, 53, 57, 59, 60	17	2, 3, 4, 6, 10, 14, 16, 17, 26, 33, 34, 37, 38, 50, 51, 59, 60	17	8, 9, 10, 13, 14, 15, 16, 19, 21, 23, 26, 27, 29, 31, 34, 35, 36, 37, 38, 49, 52, 55, 57	23	6, 7, 9, 12, 24, 26, 27, 29, 33, 39, 47, 48, 56	14
(5)	High (H)	2, 3, 7, 19, 26, 28, 30, 33, 34, 36, 38, 48, 58	13	7, 8, 11, 18, 32, 39, 48, 52, 54, 55, 57, 61, 58	13	2, 3, 7, 20, 28, 30, 32, 39, 40, 45, 56, 61	12	1, 2, 3, 8, 30, 35, 38, 55	8
(6)	Very High (VH)	11, 32, 47, 54, 55, 56	6	1, 36, 45, 46, 47, 49	6	46	1	18, 28, 31, 36, 45, 46, 57	7
(7)	Very-Very High (VVH)	1, 37, 45, 46	4	19, 20, 56	3	1, 11, 33, 47	4	19, 20, 54	3
	Missing/Total	62, 63	62	62, 63	62	58, 59, 60, 62, 63	59	58, 59, 60, 62, 63	59

Similarly, regions 11, 32 and 37 also have below average unemployment. All these regions also have below average real per capita income and region 37 is very poor on the basis of nominal income (expenditure). Region 11 (Southern Gujarat Plain) is an exception in that though nominal income is relatively high, real income is low. Thus, region 11 and 13 have high poverty despite high per capita expenditure and low employment presumably because of price factor. Because of this a very high proportion of income has to be spent on food and the ultra-poverty line is exceptionally high, consequently real income is depressed.

Quality of Life

We have used three measures of quality of life: literacy among female population, survival ratio and proportion of kutcha houses in rural area. Since these are not significantly correlated with each other, they have to be considered separately.

Among the regions of acute nutritional deficiency, regions 19, 20, 26 and 30 have very high literacy among female population. Only region 38 has very high poverty and very low female literacy (Table 4.4, col. 2). Of the other poverty stricken regions, three regions (46, 56, 62) have high literacy and five (6, 24, 32, 37, 43) have low literacy.

Among the regions with relatively low poverty on the basis of DER, regions 18 and 41 have very high illiteracy an regions 15, 17, 25 and 53 have high illiteracy. Unexpectedly, poverty and illiteracy generally do not go together in India.

The distribution of regions by illiteracy is not normal. Twenty-six regions have above average illiteracy, whereas only twelve regions have blow average. Regions 19, 20, 62, 63 and 46 have very high literacy whereas regions 10, 26, 30, 33, 39, 56 and 61 have slightly higher than average literacy. On the opposite side of the spectrum, regions 18, 32 and 41 have very high illiteracy, however, twenty three regions have high literacy.

Quality of life is also reflected by the size and quality of housing. One such measure is the percentage of kutcha houses in rural areas. Admittedly, this is an incomplete indicator, since building practices are determined to a large extent by the local natural conditions and the locally available building materials. In kutcha houses, we have included only those with kutcha walls. The distribution is platykurtic and is far from normality. Very high above average proportion of kutcha houses are found in regions 4, 36, 37, 48, 58, 1, 5, 45, 51, 57 and 59. In contrast, much below average proportion is found in regions 3, 21, 22, 31, 11, 23, 29, 49, 50 and 61.

Among the poorest regions, only regions 38 and 45 have above average proportion of kutcha houses. In fact, regions 9, 27, 30 and 31 have below average proportion of kutcha houses (Table 4.4, col. 4). Hence, housing conditions, specially the variable chosen, does not represent quality of life adequately. Rather, it reflects local geophysical and climatic conditions.

Survival ratio has been taken to be a proxy for expectation of life at birth. However, survival ratio is affected by migration streams. The distribution of regions by survival ratio is leptokurtic; most of the regions have near average survival ratio. Inter-regional variations in this ratio are quite low. Only nine regions have below average and sixteen above average value of the ratio. Thus, 38 regions have all India average survival ratio.

Of the nine very poor regions, regions 19, 26 and 45 have high to very high survival ratio and none has low or very low ratio. Amongst the poor regions, regions 32 and 62 have very high survival ratio, only regions 11 and 57 have low ratio. In contrast, of the regions with very low poverty, only regions 17 and 61 have very high survival ratio and region 53 has low ratio. Among the other low poverty regions, region 48 has high and region 52 low survival ratio.

The above regional pattern reveals that, in Indian conditions, quality of life is not a function of economic development alone. Natural conditions, quality of leadership, history, etc., influence the spread of education, longevity and other aspects of quality of life.

III
HIGHEST AND LOWEST POVERTY NUTRITIONAL INADEQUACY REGIONS

The summary poverty profiles of the ten regions with the highest and lowest poverty (nutritional inadequacy) are given in Table 4.5 and 4.6. The numbers given in the tables are the standardised scores of the respective variables. The signs of expenditure and real income scores should be reversed to indicate incidence of poverty based on income insufficiency. Col. 13 gives the standardised scores on illiteracy — showing low quality of life.

TABLE 4.4: Quality of Life: Distribution of Regions

Sl. No.	Indicators/ Categories	Female Illiteracy (FILLR)		Percentage of Rural Kutcha House (PKH)		Survival Rate (SURR)		Infant Death Rate (IMR)	
		Serial No. of Regions	f	Serial No. of Regions	f	Serial No. of Regions	f	Serial No. of Regions	f
		1	2	3	4	5	6	7	8
(1)	Very-Very Low (VVL)	19, 20, 62, 63	4	3, 21, 22, 31	4	2, 56	2	21	1
(2)	Very Low (VL)	46	1	11, 23, 29, 49, 50, 61	6	8, 10	2	20, 33	2
(3)	Low (L)	10, 26, 30, 33, 39, 56, 61	7	8, 9, 10, 13, 14, 15, 16, 17, 24, 25, 27, 30, 33, 34, 35, 42, 53, 62	18	3, 11, 52, 53, 57	5	2, 3, 9, 11, 17, 19, 35	7

(4)	Average (A)	1, 4, 9, 11, 12, 13, 14, 16, 27, 28, 31, 34, 35, 36, 40, 45, 47, 48, 49, 54, 55, 57, 64	23	2, 6, 12, 18, 19, 20, 26, 28, 39, 41, 43, 44, 46, 47, 52, 56	16	1, 4, 6, 7, 9, 12, 13, 14, 15, 16, 20, 21, 22, 23, 25, 27, 28, 29, 30, 31, 33, 34, 35, 37, 38, 39, 50, 51, 54	40	1, 10, 12, 13, 14, 15, 18, 26, 34, 36, 40, 41, 46, 47, 48	16
(5)	High (H)	2, 3, 5, 6, 7, 8, 15, 17, 21, 22, 23, 25, 29, 37, 38, 42, 43, 44, 50, 51, 52, 53	23	7, 32, 38, 40, 54, 55, 60, 63, 64	9	5, 19, 26, 48	4	22, 29, 30	3
(6)	Very High (VH)	18, 32, 41	3	1, 5, 45, 51, 57, 59	6	18, 32, 36, 62	4	25, 27	2
(7)	Very-Very High (VVH)	–	–	4, 36, 37, 48, 58	5	17, 45, 61, 64	4	23, 24, 37, 32	4
	Missing/Total	58, 59, 60	61	–	64	58, 59, 60	61		35

Highest Poverty Regions

Region 19 (Northern Kerala) and region 20 (Southern Kerala) have exceptionally high proportion of the ultrapoor population indicating heavy nutritional inadequacy. However, household budget allocation to food items is still very low. This is due to the very high income insufficiency and also land deprivation and job non-availability (URR). Disparity among the poor is also high, higher than overall disparity in the distribution of income (expenditure) and land and assets. However, illiteracy is exceptionally low, specially in region 20 indicating very very high quality of life in comparison to the other regions. This testifies to the existence of widespread, cheap and efficient education system in the region, perhaps inherited from the past when the region might not have been so poor. Despite very very high nutritional inadequacy, survival ratio is not low. Thus, multitude of factors, specially skewed distribution of land and assets and high unemployment rate (i.e., physical capital deprivation and human capital non-utilisation) are the main aspects of poverty in these two regions of Kerala.

In the case of region 27, nutritional poverty is very high, however, expenditure on food is relatively low. It also suffers from high income insufficiency. However, inequalities in the distribution of assets and income are either average or below average and unemployment rate is also at the average for all the regions. The main cause of nutritional inadequacy and insufficiency is not asset deprivation or skewed distribution of assets and income but, perhaps, low productivity.

It should be noted that the absolute standardised score of real income is much larger than that of nominal income (expenditure) in all these three regions (19, 20, 27). Thus, the poverty line expenditure is very high in these regions implying that either prices are relatively higher and/or higher priced goods form the consumption basket. Thus, the price factor makes it impossible for the rural masses to obtain the DER.

The poverty profile of region 45 is similar to that of regions, 19 and 20 in almost all details excepting asset deprivation and quality of life, though the proportions are lower: high unemployment coupled with high asset and land deprivation. Moreover, quality of life is either at the average level (literacy) or low (PKH) and both per capita nominal expenditure and real income are low. Hence people are unable to reach the DER.

TABLE 4.5: Profiles of Regions with Very High Poverty

Name of Very Poor Region		PUP	PEF	DAP	PG	SI	RY	Y(APE)	LY	AD	LD	COLA	URR	FILLR	PKH
		1	2	3	4	5	6	7	8	9	10	11	12	13	14
Northern Kerala	(19)	2.22	−1.45	1.10	2.10	2.11	−1.35	−0.61	0.72	0.47	1.77	0.37	2.39	−2.73	−0.19
Southern Kerala	(20)	2.09	−2.44	0.92	2.23	1.91	−1.29	0.00	0.75	−0.02	2.69	0.44	2.91	−4.51	−0.12
Inland Western Maharashtra	(27)	1.48	−1.59	0.24	0.95	0.98	−1.08	−0.28	−0.50	−0.06	−0.68	−0.03	0.17	−0.37	−0.92
Coastal Northern Tamil Nadu	(45)	1.42	−1.35	0.74	0.85	1.30	−0.90	−0.81	0.62	1.72	1.62	0.90	1.15	−0.17	1.40
Northern Orissa	(38)	1.40	0.21	1.28	1.28	1.65	−0.91	−1.57	1.52	0.60	−0.18	−0.25	0.50	0.52	0.76
Eastern Plains Gujarat	(9)	1.15	1.14	0.10	0.76	0.82	−0.84	−0.96	0.05	−0.17	−0.51	−0.36	−0.20	−0.17	−0.55
Eastern Maharashtra	(31)	1.13	−0.96	−0.09	0.64	0.76	−0.73	−0.38	−0.30	−0.50	−0.44	−0.12	1.16	−0.07	−1.65
Coastal Maharashtra	(26)	1.11	−0.39	1.11	0.80	1.55	−0.83	−0.56	0.79	0.79	0.29	0.09	−0.30	0.86	−0.28
Inland Eastern Maharashtra	(30)	1.06	−0.69	0.34	0.83	0.74	−0.71	−0.50	0.53	0.76	−0.91	0.66	0.63	−0.67	−0.59
Western Plain West Bengal	(57)	1.03	0.76	0.78	1.13	1.20	−0.74	−0.91	1.21	0.16	−0.93	0.35	1.12	−0.07	1.40

TABLE 4.6: Profiles of Regions with Low Poverty

Name of Region		PUP	PEF	DAP	PG	SI	RY	Y(APE)	LY	AD	LD	COLA	URR	FILLR	PKH
		1	2	3	4	5	6	7	8	9	10	11	12	13	14
Northern Punjab	(39)	1.58	2.57	1.48	0.30	1.73	3.01	2.51	0.27	0.76	0.39	0.73	0.26	0.96	0.27
Jhelum Valley	(18)	1.54	0.01	0.28	1.24	1.68	1.77	0.89	0.11	1.98	0.64	1.46	1.53	1.11	0.26
Southern U.P.	(53)	1.51	0.11	1.21	1.20	1.48	1.27	0.23	0.87	0.14	0.76	0.41	0.77	0.81	1.02
Outer Hills of J & K	(17)	1.48	0.34	1.09	1.36	1.33	0.91	0.88	1.66	2.15	0.38	1.53	1.15	1.01	0.42
Eastern Haryana	(14)	1.48	0.48	1.41	1.17	1.85	1.93	2.09	0.23	0.78	0.26	0.10	0.86	0.32	0.67
Delhi	(61)	1.42	2.69	2.45	0.81	0.30	2.52	2.14	0.23	0.40	0.61	0.92	0.78	0.67	1.63
Southern Punjab	(40)	1.41	0.12	1.22	1.17	1.59	2.29	2.77	1.92	0.91	0.40	0.60	0.98	0.02	0.41
Northern M.P.	(25)	1.39	1.08	0.08	0.73	1.41	2.41	0.83	0.37	0.83	1.09	0.72	0.99	0.91	0.70
Western Haryana	(15)	1.36	0.14	0.93	0.79	1.49	1.39	2.37	0.23	1.07	0.92	0.13	0.81	0.71	0.50
Himachal Pradesh	(16)	1.29	0.92	1.13	0.99	1.42	1.03	2.19	0.31	2.08	0.03	0.36	1.25	0.37	0.10

In region 38 (Northern Orissa), there is a very high nutritional inadequacy and the pattern is similar to that in regions 19, 20, 45. There is high nominal and real income insufficiency, quality of life is also low. The main distinguishing feature is the average land deprivation and concentration of land and assets but very high concentration of income, in fact, highest among the ten regions. Very very low nominal income coupled with very high income inequality seem to be the main aspect of rural poverty in this region. A slightly above average unemployment rate is also a contributing factor. In addition, there are very large inequalities among the poor. Hence, PG and SI which take into consideration these inequalities are also very high.

In contrast to the above picture, region 9 (Eastern Gujarat) has average disparities among the poor, average asset deprivation, average concentration of land and assets, average inequalities in income and below average land deprivation. Even then poverty is very high. This is so despite a very high budget allocation to food, primarily because of low nominal and real income.

In the case of region 31 (Eastern Maharashtra), though the poverty and income profiles are similar to those in region 9, and asset and land deprivation too are below average, unemployment rate is very high, which seems to be the main feature and cause of poverty.

Region 26 (Coastal Maharashtra) has nutritional inadequacy, income insufficiency and resource deprivation profiles similar to those in region 27. However, nominal expenditure deficiency is somewhat lower and asset deprivation a bit higher. Unemployment rate is average and illiteracy is high. The main reason of poverty is high real income insufficiency coupled with high inequalities in its distribution and high asset deprivation. Very high disparity among the poor raises PG and, more markedly, the Sen's Index.

The distinguishing feature of the poverty profile of region 30 (Inland Eastern Maharashtra) is high asset deprivation and low land deprivation but high concentration of land and assets and high unemployment rate. Thus, low and skewed distribution of income, high asset deprivation and unemployment are the main facets of the problem. Quality of life is high. A complicating factor is that households spend much less than 80 per cent of their budget on food items.

Thus, of the ten highest poverty stricken regions, very high unemployment is the main facet of poverty in five regions (19, 20, 45,

31 and 57), very high land deprivation in three regions (19, 20 and 45), asset deprivation in only region 45, low nominal expenditure/income in region 38 and to lesser extend in regions 9 and 57, low real income in regions 19, 20 and 27 and to a smaller but significant extent in all the other seven regions. Disparities among the poor is significant factor in regions 38, 19 and 26 and to a lesser extent in regions 20, 57 and 45 thereby decreasing the appropriateness of the head-count ratio as compared to poverty-gap and Sen's index as a measure of nutritional inadequacy. In regions 9 and 57, households are unable to obtain the DER despite spending a very high proportion of their total budget (well beyond 80 per cent) on food items. However, in regions 19, 20, 27, 45, 31 and 30, despite nutritional inadequacy households do not choose to spend even 80 per cent of their budget on the food items. Regions 9 and 57 are the worst sufferers on all counts — nutritional inadequacy despite very high allocation of the budget to food items, land deprivation and income insufficiency.

Lowest Poverty Regions

It will be interesting to compare the poverty profiles of the very high poverty regions with the very low poverty regions.

Region 39 (Northern Punjab) has the lowest nutritional ultrapoverty among 64 regions in India. However, the deviation from the all india average (i.e., the average for all the regions) is not as marked as in the case of the most poverty stricken region (19). Sen's index is also very low, however, poverty gap is not that low. Very low nutritional inadequacy is achieved despite much less than 80 per cent of the budget being spent on food. This is because of very very high nominal average per capita expenditure and real income, average or low inequalities in the distribution of income and assets and low unemployment rate. Quality of life is also high. However, there are large disparities of income among the poor and land deprivation and concentration of land and assets are somewhat on the higher side.

Region 61 (Delhi) is also in a low poverty situation which is almost similar to that in region 39 (Northern Punjab).

Region 18 (Jammu and Kashmir — Jhelum) is an exceptional region. It has very low poverty ratio, a 80 per cent budget allocation to food items achieved through high real income, high nominal income and very low asset deprivation and concentration of land and assets. However, there is very high unemployment as well as very high illiteracy. Unemployment is very high only in this region. In all other nine lowest poverty regions, unemployment is either low or very low.

In regions 53 (Southern U.P.), poverty is low because of very high real income, though nominal income/expenditure is average. Thus poverty line expenditure is quite low. This may be because of low prices of food items or consumption of low quality energy giving foods. The expenditure on food is nearly 80 per cent of total expenditure. Low unemployment rate coupled with low inequalities in the distribution of income, land and assets, specially among the poor, help in achieving the DER even with not so high an average per capita expenditure level. Thus dietary habits, egalitarian distribution and price factor can be identified as the main factors. Quality of life is also relatively high.

In regions 17 (Jammu and Kashmir — Outer Hills), the same factors operate even more forcefully. In regions 14 (Eastern Haryana), the price factor is not operating. Both nominal and real income are very very high, income inequalities are at the average level, asset deprivation is low but land deprivation and concentration of land and assets are high. Unemployment is low. Because of high nominal and real income and low intra-poor disparities, the low income households are able to achieve the DER with relatively very very low proportion of the budget being allocated to food items. Similar remarks hold for region 40 (Southern Punjab) with a few modifications. There is high income and unemployment is low. The main reason for low poverty seems to be very very low inequalities among the poor as well as all rural households.

In region 25 (Northern M.P.), high nominal income alongwith very high real income (favourable price and diet-composition factors) and very high allocation to food items are the main reasons of the achievement of low poverty. Low unemployment and low resource deprivation are the other helping factors. However, though resource deprivation and resource inequalities are low, this fact is not reflected in the distribution of income.

Similar remarks hold in the case of region 15 (Western Haryana) and 16 (H.P.). However, real income advantage is less than the nominal income advantage reflecting price disadvantage. Relatively very very high nominal income, low asset deprivation, low to very low unemployment rate and low inequalities among the poor are the main features of low poverty in these regions. Moreover, budget allocation to food is also low.

IV
EXCESS POVERTY

We have dealt with various indicators of poverty. The two most important indicators are per capita real income (RY) and percentage of ultrapoor in rural population (PUP). A comparison of scores on the two indicators (Table 4.7a, 4.7b and 4.8) gives an interesting reading (it may be remembered that we have to reverse the signs of standard scores on per capita real income). In general, the two scores follow closely yet there are several instances of divergence between the two. The best ten regions in accordance with per capita real income are region number 39, 61, 25, 40, 14, 18, 42, 15, 53 and 44. The best ten regions in accordance with percentage of ultrapoor are region number 39, 18, 53, 17, 14, 61, 40, 25, 15 and 16. Eight of the ten best regions are common in both the lists, and three others are also border-line cases. Similarly, the worst ten regions are 19, 20, 27, 38, 45, 9, 6, 26, 37 and 28 according to real per capita income and 19, 20, 27, 45, 38, 9, 31, 26, 30 and 57 according to percentage of ultrapoor. Some of these regions are the worst sufferers on both the counts (region number 19, 20, 27, 45, 38, 9, 26).

TABLE 4.7a: Ranking of Regions According to Real Income (RY)

Rank	Best Ten Regions		Worst Ten Regions	
	Region No.	RY-Score	Region No.	RY-Score
1.	39	3.0124	19	−1.3456
2.	61	2.5201	20	−1.2885
3.	25	2.4121	27	−1.0787
4.	40	2.2953	38	−0.9144
5.	14	1.9352	45	−0.8999
6.	18	1.7693	9	−0.8415
7.	42	1.4671	6	−0.8345
8.	15	1.3909	26	−0.8269
9.	53	1.2669	37	−0.8248
10.	44	1.0339	28	−0.8139

TABLE 4.7b: Ranking of Regions According to Nominal Income (APE)

Rank	Best Ten Regions		Worst Ten Regions	
	Region	APE-Score	Region	APE-Score
1.	40	2.7696	37	−1.7240
2.	39	2.5058	38	−1.5753
3.	15	2.3665	43	−1.2508
4.	16	2.1898	21	−1.1395
5.	61	2.1439	22	−1.0740
6.	14	2.0916	55	−1.0478
7.	11	1.9569	9	−0.9627
8.	42	0.9740	57	−0.9104
9.	58	0.9609	6	−0.8795
10.	18	0.8861	17	−0.8758

TABLE 4.8: Ranking of Regions According to PUP

Rank	Best Ten Regions		Worst Ten Regions	
	Region	PUP-Score	Region	PUP-Score
1.	39	−1.5823	19	2.2235
2.	18	−1.5438	20	2.0873
3.	53	−1.5072	27	1.4846
4.	17	−1.4851	45	1.4203
5.	14	−1.4781	38	1.4001
6.	61	−1.4245	9	1.1550
7.	40	−1.4152	31	1.1297
8.	25	−1.3954	26	1.1109
9.	15	−1.3560	30	1.0607
10.	16	−1.2898	57	1.0278

Following Sen (1980 : 12-15), we have computed excess poverty. Excess poverty is defined as the excess of poverty score over the per capita real income score (with sign changed) (Table 4.9). Some of the regions deemed to be the best according to the above two indicators are the worst performers according to the indicator of excess poverty. They are: Punjab Northern (39), M.P. Western (24), Delhi (61) and M.P. North Eastern (25). That is, they have a poverty ratio which is higher than that expected on the basis of their relatively high per capita real income level. Moreover, Kerala Northern (19) and Kerala

Southern (20) are the worst sufferers considering all the three criteria. In contrast, region Jammu and Kashmir (17) is the best on the basis of these criteria. Meghalaya (60), Manipur (58, 59), Tripura (48), Eastern U.P. (52), Assam (4, 5), Inland Eastern and Eastern Madhya Pradesh (21, 22) though not showing very low poverty, are having poverty levels much below those expected on the basis of their low level of per capita real income. Though Punjab Northern (39) and Punjab Southern (40), Delhi (61) and M.P. North-Eastern (25) have low poverty, they ought to have done considerably better on the basis of their relatively high level of development.

Analysis with nominal expenditure in place of real per capita expenditure (income) also gives nearly identical results (Table 4.10).

TABLE 4.9: Ranking of Regions According to Real Excess Poverty

Rank	Best Ten Regions		Worst Ten Regions	
	Region	Real Excess Poverty	Region	Real Excess Poverty
1.	60	−1.5913	39	1.4301
2.	58	−0.9574	24	1.0777
3.	59	−0.8914	61	1.0955
4.	48	−0.7436	25	1.0167
5.	52	−0.6180	40	0.8801
6.	5	−0.6012	19	0.8779
7.	17	−0.5744	20	0.7988
8.	21	−0.5661	23	0.6374
9.	22	−0.5088	42	0.5688
10.	4	−0.4770	45	0.5204

TABLE 4.10: Ranking of Regions According to Nominal Excess Poverty

Rank	Best Ten Regions		Worst Ten Regions	
	Region	Nominal Excess Poverty	Region	Nominal Excess Poverty
1.	17	−2.3609	11	2.8495
2.	22	−1.8906	20	2.0878
3.	53	−1.7377	19	1.6115
4.	21	−1.4914	40	1.3544
5.	51	−1.0760	27	1.2017
6.	52	−1.0386	62	1.1820
7.	44	−1.0376	15	1.0105
8.	50	−0.9794	39	0.9235
9.	59	−0.9606	16	0.8999
10.	37	−0.7342	24	0.8433

Similar analysis can be undertaken for the other indicators of poverty and quality of life.

V
POVERTY CLUSTERS

Formation of the Poverty Clusters

Cluster formation of the first 57 regions is attempted by taking four nutritional inadequacy indicators (PUP, PP, PG, SI), two income insufficiency indicators (APE, RY), two income inequality measures (DAP, LY), five resource deprivation indicators (AVA, AD, LD, COLA, URR) and three quality of life indicators (FILLR, SURR, PKH). The variables are first standardised and then an Euclidean distance matrix between the first 57 regions (57 X 57 matrix) is computed (Mather 1976 : 311-312). The cluster formation technique (Mather 1976 : 318-326) is used to derive clusters at step 10, 20, 30, 40 and 50. The cumulative error sum of squares (ESS) at steps 10, 20, 30, 40 and 50 is 0.781, 2.171, 4.110, 7.981 and 16.371 per cent respectively. Thus, the cumulative error is quite low up to the 40th step; hence the intra-cluster distance would be quite low at this step.

At step 10, nine multiple region clusters are formed, which between themselves accommodate 19 regions, thus 38 regions form isolated clusters. At step 20, three regions are added to the previous clusters and five more clusters are formed. Still twenty five regions are outside any cluster. At step 30, many new regions are added to the existing clusters and many clusters are merged. No new cluster is formed. At step 40, all but six regions enter clusters. Thus, now there are eleven multiple region clusters and six single region clusters.

It is useful to note that at step 10, the smallest intra-multi-region cluster distance is 1.44 and the highest is also only 2.50. The highest intra-cluster distances at the 20th, 30th, 40th step are 3.98, 6.39 and 11.35 respectively. The clustering scheme formed at step 50, since the cumulative ESS is high, is not used here, however, the cluster scheme at the 50th step has been used to rearrange the clusters formed at step 40. The sequence of regions in each cluster is the one in which they entered it. It is interesting to note that in many of the clusters the regions do not belong to the same state, they are not even contiguous. This indicates the existence of vast intra-state differentials in poverty. The remaining regions for which only some of the required data are available have been placed in the most appropriate clusters by inspection.

The composition of the clusters and the poverty profiles of the regions are given in Table 4.11. The following clusters can be identified.

Cluster I: Very Very High Poverty: Northern Kerala (19) and Southern Kerala (20)

These regions are characterised by very high resource deprivation, very high rural unemployment rate and very high income insufficiency and income inequality among the poor as well as total population. However, the proportion of expenditure on food is relatively low and quality of life is very high.

The following regions can be added to this cluster: Coastal Northern Tamil Nadu (45), Coastal Maharashtra (26), Coastal and Ghats of Karnataka (32), Northern Orissa (38), Western Plains of West Bengal (57), Central Plains of West Bengal (56) and Southern Orissa (37).

These regions are similar to Northern Kerala (19) and Southern Kerala (20). However, these have some minor differences. Coastal Northern Tamil Nadu (45) and Coastal Maharashtra (26) have very high asset deprivation but a bit lower inequality. However, nothing can be said with certainty about quality of life except that quality of life is high in Coastal Maharashtra (26). Coastal and Ghats of Karnataka (32) has low unemployment rate but very high poverty despite spending high proportion of budget on food items.

In Northern Orissa (38) and Western Plains of West Bengal (57), resource deprivation is average (slightly on a higher side) and percentage expenditure on food is also average.

Central Plains of West Bengal (56) is marked by very very high resource deprivation. Similarly, Southern Orissa (37) has very very high asset deprivation and high percentage expenditure on food.

Thus, in this cluster the only major intracluster difference is regarding the proportion of expenditure on food (PEF).

Cluster II: High to Very High Poverty: South Bihar (6), Eastern Gujarat (9), Northern Karnataka (35), Southern Rajasthan (43) and Eastern Maharashtra (31)

In Southern Bihar (6), Eastern Gujarat (9), and Northern Karnataka (35), resource deprivation is average but land deprivation is low.

TABLE 4.11: Poverty Profile of Regions

Cluster No.	Name of Regions		PUP	PP	PG	SI	PEF	RY	APE	LY	AVA	AD	LD	COLA	URR	FILLR	SURR	PKH	DAP
			1	2	3	4	5	6	7	8	9	10	11	12	13	14	15	16	17
1.	Coastal Andhra Pradesh	(1)	H	H	A	H	A	L	L	H	L	VVH	VH	VVH	H	A	A	VH	A
	Inland Tamil Nadu	(47)	A	A	H	H	L	A	L	A	L	VH	VH	VVH	A	A	H	A	A
	Inland Eastern Karnataka	(33)	A	A	H	H	VL	L	A	VH	A	H	A	VVH	A	L	H	L	H
	Coastal Southern Tamil Nadu	(46)	H	H	A	A	A	L	L	H	L	VVH	VH	VH	VH	VL	H	A	L
	Plains, Southern Gujarat	(11)	H	A	VH	H	VVL	L	VVH	VH	A	VH	H	VVH	L	A	L	VL	A
10.	Northern Kerala	(19)	VVH	VH	VVH	VVH	VL	VL	L	H	L	H	VVH	A	VVH	VVL	H	A	VH
14.	Coastal Maharashtra	(26)	VH	VH	H	VH	L	L	L	H	L	H	A	A	A	L	H	L	VH
	Coastal and Ghats Karnataka	(32)	H	H	H	H	H	L	A	A	L	VH	H	H	L	VH	H	H	A
	Coastal Northern Tamil Nadu	(45)	VH	VH	H	VH	VL	L	L	H	L	VVH	VH	H	VH	A	VH	VH	H
	Coastal Orissa	(36)	A	A	A	H	A	A	A	H	L	H	VH	A	VH	A	VH	VVH	H
	Himalayan West Bengal	(54)	H	H	A	H	A	L	L	A	L	VH	H	L	VVH	A	H	H	A
15.	Southern Orissa	(37)	H	H	H	H	H	A	VVL	A	VL	VVH	A	A	L	H	H	VVH	A
	Northern Orissa	(38)	VH	H	VH	VVH	A	L	VL	VH	L	H	A	A	H	H	H	H	VH
	Western Plains West Bengal	(57)	H	H	VH	VH	H	L	L	VH	L	A	H	A	VH	A	H	VH	VH
	Central Plains West Bengal	(56)	H	H	VH	VH	A	L	L	VH	L	VH	VVH	H	A	L	A	A	H
2.	Northern Bihar	(7)	A	A	A	H	H	A	L	H	L	A	A	A	A	H	A	H	A
	Central Bihar	(8)	A	A	A	A	H	A	A	H	A	A	H	A	H	H	VL	H	A
	Inland Southern Andhra Pradesh	(2)	A	A	A	A	H	L	L	A	A	H	A	H	H	H	VVL	A	A

(Contd.)

TABLE 4.11: (*Contd.*)

			1	2	3	4	5	6	7	8	9	10	11	12	13	14	15	16	17
5.	Southern Bihar	(6)	H	H	H	H	H	L	L	H	L	A	A	L	A	H	A	A	H
	Eastern Plains Gujarat	(9)	VH	H	H	H	VH	L	L	A	A	A	L	A	A	A	A	L	A
	Inland Northern Karnataka	(35)	A	A	H	H	H	L	L	H	A	A	VL	A	L	A	H	L	A
	Eastern Maharashtra	(31)	VH	VH	H	H	L	L	A	A	A	L	L	A	VH	A	H	VVL	H
	Southern Rajasthan	(43)	H	H	A	H	VH	L	VL	VVH	A	L	L	VL	VL	H	H	A	A
13.	Inland Western Madhya Pradesh	(23)	A	A	L	A	A	A	A	H	A	A	VL	A	L	H	A	VVL	A
	Inland Southern Karnataka	(34)	L	A	A	L	L	A	A	A	L	H	A	A	A	A	H	L	A
	Western Madhya Pradesh	(24)	H	A	A	A	A	A	A	H	H	L	VL	L	A	L	A	VL	A
	Inland Western Maharashtra	(27)	VH	VH	H	H	VL	VL	A	L	A	A	L	A	A	A	A	A	A
	Inland Northern Maharashtra	(28)	H	H	H	VH	L	L	L	A	A	H	L	H	VH	A	A	L	H
	Inland Eastern Maharashtra	(30)	VH	H	H	H	L	L	L	H	A	H	L	H	H	L	A	VL	A
	Inland Central Maharashtra	(29)	A	H	H	H	A	A	A	H	A	A	VL	A	A	L	A	A	VVH
3.	Inland Southern Andhra Pradesh	(3)	A	A	H	H	A	A	A	H	L	H	A	H	H	H	L	VVL	H
4.	Plains Assam	(4)	A	H	A	A	A	L	L	VL	L	A	A	VL	L	A	A	VVL	L
	Hills Assam	(5)	A	H	L	A	L	L	L	VL	L	L	L	VL	VL	H	H	VL	L
	Tripura	(48)	L	L	A	L	H	A	VVH	L	L	H	H	L	A	A	H	VVH	L
	Central Uttar Pradesh	(51)	L	L	L	L	A	H	VVL	A	L	A	A	VL	L	H	H	VVH	L
6.	Dry Areas of Gujarat	(12)	A	H	A	A	H	A	A	L	H	L	VL	L	A	A	A	A	L
	Saurashtra Gujarat	(13)	A	H	A	L	H	L	A	L	VVH	A	L	A	L	A	A	L	L
	Plains Northern Gujarat	(10)	A	A	L	L	VH	A	H	A	H	L	A	A	L	L	VL	L	L
	Western Rajasthan	(41)	VL	L	L	VL	VVH	H	H	A	H	L	VL	VL	L	VH	H	A	L

(*Contd.*)

TABLE 4.11: (*Contd.*)

			1	2	3	4	5	6	7	8	9	10	11	12	13	14	15	16	17
12.	South Eastern Rajasthan	(44)	L	VL	L	VL	A	VH	A	A	H	VL	VL	L	VL	H	H	A	L
	Eastern Uttar Pradesh	(52)	L	L	L	L	H	A	L	L	L	L	H	A	L	H	H	A	L
	Western Uttar Pradesh	(50)	L	L	L	L	A	H	A	A	H	L	A	L	L	H	H	VL	L
	Southern Uttar Pradesh	(53)	VL	VL	VL	VL	A	VH	A	L	L	A	A	VL	L	H	H	L	VL
	Inland Eastern M.P.	(22)	L	A	L	L	VH	A	VL	L	L	A	L	L	L	H	A	VVL	L
	Himalayan Uttar Pradesh	(49)	A	A	A	A	VH	A	A	L	A	L	VH	L	VL	A	H	VL	L
	Eastern Madhya Pradesh	(21)	A	A	A	A	VH	A	VL	A	L	A	L	A	L	H	A	VVL	A
7.	Eastern Haryana	(14)	VL	VL	VL	VVL	L	VVH	VVH	A	VVH	L	A	A	L	A	A	L	VL
	Western Haryana	(15)	VL	VVL	L	VL	A	VH	VVH	A	VVH	VL	L	A	L	H	A	L	L
	Himachal Pradesh	(16)	VL	VL	L	VL	L	VH	VVH	A	H	VVL	A	A	A	A	A	L	VL
	Southern Punjab	(40)	VL	VVL	VL	VL	A	VVH	VVH	VVL	VVH	L	L	H	L	A	H	H	VL
16.	Northern Punjab	(39)	VL	VVL	A	VVL	VVH	VVH	VVH	A	VVH	L	H	H	A	L	H	L	VH
8.	Outer Hills of J&K	(17)	VL	VL	VL	VL	A	H	L	VVL	H	VVL	A	VL	VL	H	VVH	L	VL
9.	Northern Madhya Pradesh	(25)	VL	VVL	L	VL	VH	VVH	H	A	A	L	VL	L	L	H	A	L	A
	North Eastern Rajasthan	(42)	L	VL	L	VL	A	VH	H	VL	H	VL	VL	L	L	H	H	L	VL
	Jhelum Valley of J&K	(18)	VL	VVL	VL	VVL	A	A	H	A	A	VVL	H	VL	VH	VH	VH	A	A
11.	Southern Kerala	(20)	VVH	VH	VVH	VVH	VVL	VL	A	H	L	A	VVH	H	VVH	VVL	A	A	H
17.	Eastern Plains of West Bengal	(55)	H	H	VH	VH	VH	L	VL	VH	L	VH	H	A	H	A	H	H	H
	Regions not included in the cluster exercise																		
	Plain Manipur	(58)	L	A	VL	L	H	A	L	VVL	L	H	H	—	—	—	—	VVH	VL
	Hill Manipur	(59)	L	A	VL	VL	VH	VH	A	L	L	A	A	—	—	—	—	VH	VL
	Meghalaya	(60)	L	H	L	L	VL	L	L	VVL	L	A	A	—	—	—	—	H	VL
	Delhi	(61)	VL	VL	L	A	VVL	VVH	VVH	A	VVH	L	H	—	—	L	VVH	VL	L
	Goa, Daman Diu	(62)	H	VH	A	H	A	L	A	L	—	—	—	—	—	VVL	VH	L	VVH
	Pondicherry	(63)	A	H	A	A	VL	A	A	A	—	—	—	—	L	VVL	A	L	H
	J & K Mountaneous	(64)	—	—	—	—	—	—	—	—	H	VVL	L	—	VL	A	VVH	H	—

Unemployment rate is average. There is high income insufficiency as well as high inequalities in income. Quality of life is average. However, poverty is high despite high percentage of expenditure on food.

In Southern Rajasthan (43), the profile is similar except that income inequalities are very high and rural unemployment rate is very low. In contrast, in Eastern Maharashtra (31), income inequalities are average but unemployment is very high.

Cluster III: High to Very High Poverty: Inland Northern Maharashtra (28), Inland Central Maharashtra (29), Inland Western Maharashtra (27) and Inland Eastern Maharashtra (30)

This cluster is characterised by average to high asset deprivation, low land deprivation but high rural unemployment rate and high income insufficiency with average income inequality. However, percentage expenditure on food is low. In Inland Central Maharashtra region (29), the profile is slightly different — all the poverty measures show lower values compared to the other three regions. Despite this, poverty is high because of very high inequalities in income distribution among the poor as well as the total population. The households also spend about 80 per cent of the budget on food items.

Cluster IV (A): Average to High Poverty: Coastal Andhra Pradesh (1), Inland Tamil Nadu (47), Inland Eastern Karnataka (33), Coastal Southern Tamil Nadu (46)

The following regions can also be added to this cluster:

Southern Gujarat Plains (11), Coastal Orissa (36) and Himalayan West Bengal (54).

There is high to very high resource deprivation, very high to average rural unemployment rate, high income insufficiency and income inequalities and average quality of life. Poverty is high but percentage of expenditure on food is low. In the case of Coastal Southern Tamil Nadu (46), the only major differences are that rural unemployment rate is very high but still quality of life is high. Nutritional poverty is high despite the fact that 80 per cent of average expenditure is on food.

In Southern Gujarat Plains (11), rural unemployment rate is low and percentage expenditure on food is also very very low. There is price disadvantage in this region. In Coastal Orissa (36) and Himalayan West Bengal (54), rural unemployment rate is very high, quality of life is average and percentage expenditure on food is average which is still high at 80 per cent. The poverty situation is, therefore, not easy.

Cluster IV (B): High Poverty: Eastern Plains of West Bengal (55)

In Eastern Plains of West Bengal (55), the asset base is low but resource deprivation is high. Rural unemployment rate, income insufficiency and income inequality are high. All these lead to high poverty ratio despite a very high percentage of expenditure on food.

Cluster V: Average Poverty: Northern Bihar (7), Central Bihar (8), Inland Northern Andhra Pradesh (2), Inland Southern Andhra Pradesh (3)

In this cluster, asset deprivation is average, however, land deprivation is high, rural unemployment rate is high, income insufficiency is average tending towards high and income inequality is also high. Quality of life is low. However, poverty is average achieved by high budget allocation to food. Hence the average poverty scenario is deceptive. In Inland Southern Andhra Pradesh (3), the poverty indicator is sensitive to the formula used, this may be because of high disparity among the poor (DAP). In addition, in this region, resource deprivation is high. Thus, the average poverty scenario seems to be deceptive.

Cluster VI: Average Poverty: Assam Plains (4) and Assam Hills (5)

Regions in this cluster have average to low resource deprivation and low rural unemployment rate. Still they have high income insufficiency and high inequalities, because of these there is average nutritional poverty; quality of life is also average. Other variables are at average level.

Cluster VII: Average Poverty: Inland Western Madhya Pradesh (23), Inland Southern Karnataka (34), Western M.P. (24) and Pondicherry (63)

Nearly all variables are at average level, land deprivation is very low.

Hence, nutritional poverty is at the average level. Of the four regions, region 34 is the best and region 24 the worst.

Cluster VIII (A): Average Poverty: Dry Areas of Gujarat (12), Saurashtra Gujarat (13) and Northern Gujarat Plains (10)

These regions have very high value of assets, low asset and low resource deprivation, low to average rural unemployment rate, average income, low income inequality and average quality of life. However, despite this favourable resource and income situation, poverty is at the all India average level. This is in spite of high percentage of expenditure on food. This seems to be an exceptional situation.

Cluster VIII (B): Very Low Poverty: Western Rajasthan (41)

This region has profile similar to that in cluster VIII (A) except that percentage of expenditure on food is very high and quality of life is very low. However, in contrast to the dry areas of Gujarat (12), Saurashtra Gujarat (13) and Northern Gujarat Plains (10), nutritional poverty is very low. This situation creates doubts on the quality of N.S.S. consumption and expenditure data, specially on non-food items.

Cluster IX: Average Poverty: Inland Eastern Madhya Pradesh (22), Himalayan Uttar Pradesh (49) and Eastern Madhya Pradesh (21)

Regions in this cluster have low resource deprivation, low rural unemployment rate, very high nominal income, but average real income showing price disadvantage, low inequalities. Despite these factors, nutritional poverty is average even though percentage of expenditure on food is very high. Quality of life is also low.

Regions in cluster VIII and IX seem to be traditional peasant economies. With economic development, inequalities in the distribution of assets and income might increase and, hence, the poverty situation may worsen.

Cluster X: Low Poverty: South Eastern Rajasthan (44), Eastern Uttar Pradesh (52), Southern Uttar Pradesh (53), and Western Uttar Pradesh (50)

These regions have low resource deprivation, low unemployment rate, average income but high real income, evidencing price advantage, average income inequality but low disparity among the poor. All these make for low nutritional poverty with average percentage expenditure on food. However, quality of life is low.

Cluster XI: Low Poverty: Tripura (48), Central Uttar Pradesh (51), Manipur Plains (58), Manipur Hills (59)

These regions have low asset base but average resource deprivation, average to low rural unemployment rate, average income but average to low income inequalities. However, poverty is low because budget allocation to food is on higher side. In Manipur Plains (58) and Manipur Hills (59), inequalities in income distribution are low to very low.

Meghalaya (60) can also be included in this cluster. However, in this region income is low but inequalities are very low, hence poverty is low. This is achieved with proportionately very low budget allocation to food items.

Cluster XII: Very-Very Low Poverty: Eastern Haryana (14), Western Haryana (15), Himachal Pradesh (16), Northern Punjab (39), Southern Punjab (40), Outer Hills of Jammu and Kashmir (17) and Delhi (61)

These regions have very sound asset base, average to very low resource deprivation, low rural unemployment rate, very-very high income, low to very low income inequalities and average quality of life. Percentage expenditure on food is average. Thus, all these factors help in reducing poverty to a very-very low level.

In Southern Punjab (40), income inequalities are very-very low. However, in Northern Punjab (39), there is very high disparity among the poor. Quality of life is high. Low poverty ratio is achieved with very-very low percentage expenditure on food.

Outer Hills of Jammu and Kashmir (17) have similar profile to that of Eastern Haryana (14), Himachal Pradesh (16) and Southern Punjab (40). Though nominal income is low, real income is high. Thus, there is price advantage. In addition, income inequalities are very-very low. These all lead to very low poverty. In Delhi (61), the only difference with other members is that it has very-very high quality of life and very-very low budget allocation to food. These are expected in the highly urbanised capital region of India.

Cluster XIII: Very Low Poverty: Northern Madhya Pradesh (25), Northern Eastern Rajasthan (42), Jhelum Valley of Jammu and Kashmir (18)

These regions have average asset base with very low resource deprivation, low rural unemployment rate, very high real income, price advantage, average inequalities — all leading to very low nutritional poverty with average percentage expenditure on food. In the Jhelum Valley of Jammu and Kashmir, the percentage expenditure on food is high.

Note: 1. Nutritional poverty could not be calculated in the case of Jammu and Kashmir, Mountaneous (64) due to data inconsistency. However, other information is available. The region has good asset base and low resource deprivation, very low unemployment rate, quality of life is very high though literacy is average. On all these counts, nutritional poverty is also expected to be quite low. The region can be put in either Cluster XII or Cluster XIII.

2. Several data about the region Goa, Daman and Diu (62) are not available. This region has got average asset base, average income, slight price advantage, low overall income inequalities but very high disparities among the poor. Though quality of life is very high poverty is also high. One of the reasons may be a below average budget allocation to food items. Energy requirements might also be low.

VI
CONCLUSIONS

The poverty situation in regions of India is highly differentiated. Moreover, the classification of regions into poverty categories is not unique. It varies with the criterion chosen for defining poverty. Even though the ordinal ranking of regions by nutritional inadequacy (poverty) is not sensitive to the particular DER norm preferred or the formula used to compute the poverty index, it is extremely sensitive to the definition of poverty in terms of alternative criteria like food inadequacy, income insufficiency, resource deprivation and quality of life. Thus the poverty pattern obtained by L.R. Jain and associates (1988 : 2395-2408) on the basis of a uniform poverty line expenditure and that obtained by us on the basis of a uniform calorie norm applied directly to each region do not have one to one correspondence. So is the case with the different indicators used by us.

If we take all these criteria and indicators simultaneously and classify the regions into few internally homogeneous clusters, then interesting patterns follow. Some regions are low poverty regions on almost all counts (cluster XII, XIII) and some are high poverty regions on almost all criteria (cluster IVB, V, III). However, some regions are having high nutritional poverty but low poverty on the basis of one or the other criteria (cluster I, II). Thus, taking the DER based food inadequacy measure as surrogate measure of poverty cannot do justice to all the regions.

The priority regions should be chosen on the basis of all these indicators and not on the basis of the so called poverty line alone. From this point of view, regions in clusters II, III, IVB and V ought to receive utmost attention. Another fact to be noted is that households in many of the hard poverty cases in terms of food deficiency do not spend adequate part of income on food items. Thus, it seems that they are undernourished by choice. And they are not poorer in terms of health and education as revealed by the quality of life indicators. In fact, seven of top ten poverty regions fall in this category. Either there is something wrong with their consumption data or the national DER requirement is too high for them — their dietary requirements are far below the one used for defining the poverty line — or the food inadequacy situation in temporary. Hence, their poverty situation is not as bad as indicated by the poverty ratio. On the contrary, the average or low poverty situation in some of the regions is deceptive since it is achieved with low income level and very high budget allocation to food items (cluster V, VIII and IX).

Northern Orissa and Eastern Gujarat Plains are the most poor regions on any criterion. Other problem regions are those in cluster II, III, IV and V. Kerala is high on the quality of life indicators and spends less on food. But it is poor on the basis of almost all other criteria. Its poverty situation is overestimated by the usual DER based poverty index.

NOTES

1. It should be mentioned that here average scores refer to the unweighted average of the scores of regions, irrespective of their size. They are not the all India average levels.
2. In the rest of the chapter, poverty is used to refer to the usual Head-Count ratio which represents only nutritional inadequacy.

5

A STUDY OF POVERTY AND ITS CORRELATES

In Section I, the nature of the relationships of poverty with structural and other variables related to the rural economy is discussed and, in Section II, hypotheses about these relationships are stated and tested with regional data.

I
VARIABLES EXPLAINING POVERTY

We have already seen that there are vast regional differentials in the prevalence of poverty, howsoever defined and measured. In this chapter, we present an analysis of the factors explaining these differentials in two of the measures of poverty discussed in the previous chapters — nutritional inadequacy and income insufficiency — in the various regions in India.

Since poverty levels in different regions are different, there must be some basic factors causing these differentials. Instead of taking all the relevant variables in one single multivariate equation to study the regional variation in poverty, it is advisable to study it in relation to different blocks of variables, each block representing a particular aspect of the economic situation and economic structure. Wherever, necessary and feasible, composite indicators of closely related variables have been developed and used in regression analysis.

Ordinary least squares method is applied to explain poverty by a wide set of variables. We know that many of the variables may be interdependent and dependent on poverty measure chosen for analysis. Thus, if per capita income or expenditure is taken as the dependent variable and survival ratio or infant mortality are taken as explanatory variables, then the problem of simultaneity bias in the estimators in OLS is likely to arise because of neglecting reverse causation, i.e. the effect of low income (poverty) on mortality and survival chances. This would necessitate the specification of simultaneous equation relationships. However, this would have taken us into model building of the entire economy requiring the use of many more variables which are not available at the regional level. Hence while interpreting the results the existence of simultaneity bias in the obtained results will have to kept in mind.

As far as possible, purely descriptive variables have been excluded from the list of explanatory variables and only the variables assumed to cause poverty have been included.

As already mentioned, our data pertain to the year 1972-73 for 64 regions of India. The results could not be updated in the absence of publication of NSS data about regions for periods after it. However, state level data are available. The state level regression results may be different from the regional level results because regional differentials might be netted out by aggregation. We shall refer to these results of a later date, whenever appropriate.[1]

Geophysical Conditions

Geophysical and climatic conditions have a bearing on the agricultural and other economic activities in many ways. These variables determine the population settlement pattern and density of population leading ultimately to increased pressure on land. However, initial favourable geophysical conditions may also lead to a prosperous diversified economy. The relationship between the geophysical conditions and economic development, and also with poverty incidence, is thus open-ended.[2] No unambiguous hypothesis can be advanced. However, it can be hypothesised that, if population size has not reached the saturation point, regions with high soil ranking and assured and widespread rainfall are expected to have lower incidence of poverty.

Forces of Production in Agriculture: Infrastructure and Inputs

Agricultural development depends on geophysical conditions and development of infrastructure and technology and availability of modern farm inputs. However, generally these variables are highly correlated. Hence, only some of the variables need to be used. Some forms of infrastructure development are class-specific, e.g.

energisation of wells. It would be interesting to see the effect of relatively higher development of class-specific infrastructure on the incidence of poverty.

It can be hypothesised that development of infrastructure has positive effect on agricultural output and productivity, however, it cannot be asserted with equal certainty that this will also reduce poverty. There is no unambiguous evidence in support of the trickle-down effect.

As already pointed out, income generation depends on the total resource (and capital) base of the households. There is no direct data on capital base at regional level. However, data about total assets, value of land, livestock, implements and equipment is available from the All India Debt and Investment Survey of the R.B.I.

It can be hypothesised that, other things remaining same, regions where infrastructure is more developed and where households have larger capital base, will have higher average incomes, specially agricultural incomes, and low poverty (Rao, 1986). However, other things are not the same. The distribution of gains will be affected by the distribution of assets and accessibility to infrastructure. Regions where large number of rural households are deprived of land and/or capital resources will have higher proportion of the poor.

Agricultural Production and Productivity and Poverty

In the absence of information about the nature of agrarian relations and the mode of exploitation, no firm hypothesis can be advanced about the effect of agricultural production and productivity on poverty. However, it is generally expected that higher output per capita and per hectare would be associated with lower poverty. Agricultural instability also hits the poorest sections of the population most severely. Hence, instability prone regions are expected to show a higher poverty-ratio.

Ahluwalia's analysis (1978) of the period 1956-57 to 1973-74 indicates a significant relationship between the percentage of rural population under poverty line and the index of agricultural production per head. His state-wise analysis is not so conclusive. Saith's (1981) findings support Ahluwalia's conclusions about the relationship, though, in contrast to him, Saith finds the overall trend in poverty to be increasing. Griffin and Ghose (1979) and Mundle (1983) find no evidence to support the trickle-down hypothesis. In contrast to these time-series all India studies, Bardhan (1981) finds in the cross-sectional study of West Bengal that the two are positively correlated. Thus, nothing conclusive can be said about the relationship. (Bardhan 1986:195).

Agricultural Growth : The Trickle Down Hypothesis

Trickle down effects of growth on poverty are emphasised by those persons who find radical institutional changes politically disturbing or unfeasible. However, the evidence on trickle down hypothesis for rural India is not unambiguous (Bardhan, 1984:189). In an inter-state model, Bardhan finds that the conclusion is not unambiguous.

Krishnaji examines the relationship between rural poverty, agricultural growth and price level. The work started with Dharm Narain. Krishnaji challenges Dharam Narain's calculations and conclusions. The high correlation is caused by the highly correlated trends in different prices used in defining the variables. (Krishnaji, N. 1987:A-78) His views are challenged by Ranade (1988 : 805-808).

Lakdawala (1978) connected the incidence of poverty in rural areas to agricultural performance through 'employment' variable. Bardhan conducted cross-section studies of the relation of rural poverty with agricultural growth at three levels of aggregation—A study of households in West Bengal, an inter-state analysis, and inter-regional analysis at one point of time (Bardhan, 1982, 1986). Bardhan finds that the probability of an agricultural labourer or primarily cultivator household falling below poverty line seems to be higher if the household is in a region where agricultural production has grown at a faster rate. (Bardhan, 1982, 1986:84, 87).

Srinivasan points out that this result will not be inconsistent with the trickle-down hypothesis if the faster growing districts have above average poverty in the initial year. (Srinivasan, 1986:52). Bardhan points out the fact that faster agricultural growth is in general helpful in alleviating poverty, but big farmer dominated growth dependent on private ownership need not be so. (Bardhan, 1982:18).

Economic Growth and Poverty

Two diametrically opposite views regarding the effect of economic growth on poverty are usually held. The optimistic position is that the poor participate in economic growth and therefore, absolute poverty is reduced. Hence maximum attention ought to be given to growth. Nothing with certainty is suggested about the direction of change in inequality in income distribution due to economic growth.

The pessimistic position is that, in atleast the initial period, the poor do not usually participate in economic growth and most poor do not benefit from it. (Griffin, 1977 quoted by Fields 1989: 174). It is asserted that "Development is accompanied by an absolute as well as relative decline in the average income of the very poor". (Adelman and Morris, 1973:3, 189) Ahluwalia and Fields refute this assertion. They found that poverty is likely to decrease rapid economic growth.

Land and Other Assets

Land is the most important asset on the basis of which subsistence and income is obtained. Not only this, land is limited, its quality varies widely and its distribution is highly skewed. In Indian conditions, where employment off the land is very limited, specially in rural areas, availability of land is the most important factor influencing the poverty situation. Poverty situation can be hypothesised to be quite severe in regions in which a large proportion of population is deprived of adequate quantity of land and pressure on land (POL) is high. In fact, the landless are more prone to be poor after controlling for caste (Lanjouw and Stern, 1991·^3-56).

Besides land, other productive assets are also distributed very unequally. This is likely to accentuate the problem of poverty.

Leasing Activities

Leasing activities may ease the situation caused by land and asset deprivation if leasing-out is from the relativey better-off households to the poorest ones and is on non-exploitative terms. Leasing-out activities are resorted to by not only the better-off households but also by the poor households, if wage work is available. However, leasing-out by the poor households is often made under distress conditions. Hence, in these conditions, leasing may increase poverty. Marked leasing-out by the large land-owners is a sure sign of feudal exploitation. This is bound to increase poverty. (Mehta and Prashad 1988: ch.3). Similarly, leasing-in by small and marginal farmers on share of crop is also an indicator of feudal relations. The effect of leasing activities on the economic conditions of the poor can, however, be studied only in relation to the debt situation.[3]

Agricultural Labour, Marginal and Small Farmers

Most rural poor and poorest among the poor are agricultural labourers, mainly landless agricultural labour households (Dandekar and Rath 1971; Vaidyanathan 1974). However, Sushma Sagar and associates contradict the result using data on Rajasthan (1987:A-70-76). They find small and marginal farmers to be equally poverty stricken.

They have used data drawn from NSS reports, rural enquiry reports, agricultural census, and population census reports. The results are quite surprising. "These data surely do not confirm the hypothesis that the poorest rural groups are the wage labour households. Secondly, it shows the small cultivator households in an inferior position to that of wage labour households", (Sagar, Ahuja, Sagar, 1987:A-70).[4] The agricultural labour households received a significantly higher average income in comparison to all rural households. This is in contrast to the all India pattern. Scheduled castes and scheduled tribes are often classified as economically backward. The results imply that–

(1) Inter-class inequalities are neutral to the social class of the landowner. Generally, they increase with average size.
(2) It cannot be said that these two sections portray the depressed classes. Consumption levels of significant number of labour households are higher than those of the other sections of population.
(3) Categorisation of economic status on the basis of assets alone cannot truly reflect economic welfare of rural masses presumed to be in poverty. (Sagar, Ahuja, Sagar 1987: A-70-76).

Unemployment and Casual Labourers

Pravin Visaria (1980) in his World Bank Staff Working Paper studies the relation between poverty and unemployment especially with respect to Gujarat and Maharashtra. He uses various definitions of unemployment. The first estimate is that of week-long unemployment. The second one is based on usual activities and is termed chronically unemployed persons. The third is based on the time disposition data and the fourth one is the major activity approach. He uses the fourth measure in discussing the data for Gujarat and Maharashtra (Visaria, 1980, 2-4). The data pertain to 27th round (1972-73) of the NSS.

Monthly per capita expenditure of households is widely used as index of poverty. Visaria has tabulated the 27th round data of unemployment for six discrete monthly per capita expenditure (MPCE) intervals. He finds a clear inverse association between MPCE and the incidence of unemployment in all sub-rounds in both rural and urban areas of the country. (Visaria, 1981: 9) However, no consistent relationship is found in terms of usual or current activity based unemployment rate. (Visaria, 1981:13).

These findings differ from the earlier indications of little association between poverty and unemployment or even a direct relationship between MPCE and the incidence of unemployment.[5] There is, thus no linear relationship between the two. (Sharma 1985:51).

It has been argued by Lakdawala (1977) that unemployment in different regions of rural India does not seem to be related to the productivity of land. According to Visaria, for 56 regions of rural India, positive correlation of 0.30 is observed between unemployment and average agricultural output per hectare. Thus, the value of agricultural output per hectare is not a good indicator of the extent of poverty in regions. (Visaria 1980:14).

"Our data for Gujarat and Maharashtra provide the first direct evidence to explain why several labour force and unemployment surveys have provided very low estimates of unemployment for rural India, lower than what many analysts consider plausible. Our disaggregated estimates of unemployment for different categories of the usually employed take account of underemployment within the reference week and are, therefore, more comprehensive than the earlier estimates that were based on the priority rule. If the impression that the rural self-employed and family workers (who account for over 50 per cent of the rural labour force) suffer from a significant level of unemployment and/or underemployment is correct, they are much less willing to search or to report their search and/or availability for work than are the employees. Further, the data are consistent with some [illegible]tive evidence provided by small-scale village surveys in which farmers indicated a distinct unwillingness to work outside their own farms. Thus, the composition of the rural working force, with a predominance of the self-employed and unpaid family helpers, is an important explanation for the low estimates of rural unemployment" (Visaria 1980:23).

Unemployment, Casual Labourers and Poverty

A very close relationship can be expected between reported level of unemployment and the proportion of casual labourers among the usually employed. Visaria finds that the coefficient of correlation between the two in rural areas of the 17 states lies between 0.82 and 0.90. In urban areas, correlation is significant but the level is much lower (Visaria, 1980, 24). In rural areas, a large majority of casual labourers (over 84%) are agricultural households. He finds that the causal labourers are obviously poor with respect to the most important asset in rural areas. They are also far behind other workers with respect to human capital. They are somewhat younger than other workers and have very low per capita expenditure. The casual labourers seem to be particularly disadvantaged group both in rural and urban areas (Visaria, 1980:27, 31-32, Lanjouw and Stern, 1991: 23-56).

Rural Debt and Credit Relations

Cash dues outstanding (debt) by its source and purpose of taking it, in conjunction with other structural and geophysical variables, help in explaining the regional differences in the prevalence of poverty in the rural areas. It is a stock variable. Indebtedness may, however, indicate mutually opposing agrarian relations — on the one hand, semi-feudal agrarian relations and on the other hand, emergence of capitalist relations. In the first case, borrowing is primarily distress borrowing taken in small sums for meeting out household deficits. Such loans are taken mainly from professional moneylenders, landlords and traders. They are self perpetuating. This may cause bondage and usurious and other forms of exploitation which would necessarily raise poverty further. The households are caught in the vicious circle of poverty and indebtedness. In this situation, the amount of debt is low. However, because of poor asset-base, the debt/asset ratio will be high. In the second case, larger dues outstanding may indicate greater credit worthiness as well as larger credit availability. Obviously, the purpose of taking such loans would be to invest in farm and non-farm business. Hence, dues outstanding per household will be relatively large, specially in the context of the credit intensive strategy of agricultural development. The predominant source of credit will be institutional agencies and agricultural moneylenders. In some cases, landlords may also provide finances. Hence, the relationship between dues outstanding and poverty can be hypothesized to be negative in such cases. However, several other combinations are possible.

Debt-credit market conditions are interlocked with land ownership, lease market and labour market conditions. These interlocked markets create diverse economic situations. Hence, all these variables should not be considered in isolation from one another.[6]

Socially Oppressed Classes and Poverty

Tribal people and persons belonging to the former untouchable castes are usually the poorest groups in rural areas. This is so because they have experienced centuries of exploitation, low production and low income. This is generally true of the scheduled castes. (Lanjouw and Stern, 1991: 23-56). Most of the tribal people live in remote areas outside the mainstream. They are generally engaged in hunting and gathering forest products. Hence, regions with high proportion of socially backward classes, represented by the proportion of scheduled castes and scheduled tribes, in the total population are expected to exhibit higher poverty.

Gender Bias

Bina Agrawal explores the interlinkages between gender, poverty and agricultural growth in India. She finds systematic bias against women and female children of poor rural households. She also finds significant cross-regional differences in the extent of this bias, which is much more pronounced in the north western states relative to the southern states. She notes that life expectancy among females is not only lower than that of males, the difference is increasing. This is reflected in the continuously declining sex-ratio (female population per thousand of male population) in India as a whole and in most of states (Agrawal, 1986: 172, 173). In nine out of fifteen states, the ratio of female to male mortality in the age-group of zero to four is greater than one (Agrawal, 1986: 197). This trend is supplemented with son-preference. Hence, bias against female child birth and rearing would be reflected in a lower sex ratio.

After examining the social cultural and economic factors working against women, she examines the relationship between female-headed households and poverty. She puts to scrutiny the analysis of the relationship by Visaria and Visaria (1983) and concludes that "female-headed" households relative to male-headed households have poorer survival chances given their lower control over land resources and their greater dependency on wage income, their rate of involuntary unemployment and lower levels of education and literacy of the households. Thus, the female-headed households are more poverty prone (Agrawal, 1986:189). This is supported by a study by Parthasarathy (1982) of a district in Andhra Pradesh.

Though, female-headed households (FH) are expected to be poorer, intra-household bias against women is expected to be less in such households and, hence, female mortality as compared to male mortality (F/M DR) would be lower in them and sex-ratio (SR) would be higher. This, in fact, is the relationship when state level data about these variables are used. Coefficient of correlation between female headedness and sex-ratio and F/M death rate ratio are 0.22 and –0.42, respectively, and that between sex-ratio and F/M death rate –0.81. (Mehta, 1990).

However, at region level, data about FH and F/M DR could not be collected. In this situation, high sex-ratio can be taken to stand for female-headedness and low F/M mortality. Regions with high sex-ratio should, therefore, exhibit high poverty. High sex-ratio is, however, not a very close proxy for female-headedness. High sex-ratio may push up (not necessarily causing) poverty because of higher proportion of nutritionally neglected sections, i.e. women. In that case, however, the higher poverty ratio will not be necessarily caused by low income or output.

Settlement of Population and Population Growth

Rural settlement pattern is a result of geo-physical conditions and agricultural development in the past. However, small scattered villages raise costs of communication, transport and development of the infrastructure, hence they can be expected to be less developed and less dynamic. Isolated village labour markets keep rural wages and incomes low (Bardhan, 1984,86:181). In arid areas, village size is large, but the villages are widely dispersed. Thus, diverse patterns are possible. They should be studied in conjunction with density of population and indicators of agricultural development.

The situation can be redeemed to some extent if there are large urban centres in the region which, even when they do not provide increased employment opportunity, pull up rural wages by opening up the rural economy, specially the rural labour markets. (Rao et al. 1986).

Some regions are experiencing quite rapid population growth. In some cases, this may be a direct result of the accelerated pace of economic development in the area leading to large influx of migrants. However, in many cases, population may increase more rapidly only because of control of epidemics and better distribution of essential items. This implies that the region is essentially in the early stages of demographic transition. This will be reflected in the high *dependency* ratio. If this population pressure is coupled with high population density then it can be expected to lead to high poverty levels.

Physiological density, defined as persons per sq. km of net sown area, is a better index of population pressure than the usually calculated density of population. In basically agrarian economies, higher density of population indicates larger pressure of population on land and thus more fragmentation of land, subsistence farming and deficit households. However, density may give misleading picture, since in states with low density of population, the geo-physical conditions may not be suitable for agriculture and human habitation.

Multivariate Models

The variables considered above interact among themselves, hence multivariate models would be more appropriate.

Rao and associates present a study of the impact of selected infrastructural, institutional and technological variables on rural poverty and inequality in consumer expenditure based on 1972-73 data for 59 national sample survey regions (Rao et al 1986:95-109).

They take a norm of 2200 calorie per capita per day. Alternatively, the poverty ratio is derived on the basis of Rs. 15 per capita per month, at the 1960-61 price level. This is converted to

1972-73 prices on the basis of state price indices for agricultural labourers. The Gini coefficient ratio pertaining to consumer expenditure is also used as dependent variable.

The explanatory variables are divided into three sub-groups:

(a) Institutional variables consisting of (i) percentage of Scheduled Caste and Scheduled Tribe population in rural population, (ii) Degree of urbanisation, and (iii) Rural literacy;
(b) Infrastructural-technological variables consisting of (1) Road density, (2) Gross irrigation ratio, (3) Canal irrigation ratio, (4) Proportion of villages electrified, and (5) Consumption of fertilisers per hectare; and
(c) Variables pertaining to growth and productivity consisting of (1) Crop output (2) Productivity per hectare (3) Consumer price index for agricultural labourers.

The 59 regions are the then divided into four broad geographic areas — the Hills, the Great Plain, the Deccan Plateau and the Coastal Areas. This is done because the impact on the level of infrastructural development may be area-specific. Log-linear relations are taken. The authors find that the regression results are somewhat sensitive to the definition of poverty. The relations of poverty with the variables are complex, though in most of the cases the results follow the usual hypotheses. In general, poverty is low in regions where urbanisation is high and unemployment is low. However, it is positively correlated to fertiliser consumption which is puzzling result. There is possibility of spurious correlation because of errors in variables.

The most glaring deficiency of the above work is that it does not take into consideration the indicators of agrarian relations and other structural variables. Again, the authors have completely neglected development in non-agricultural sectors and non-rural areas. As Dantwala has pointed out, a substantial increase in agricultural (or food) production is a necessary but not a sufficient condition for alleviation of poverty (Dantwala, 1986: 122).

In this respect, Bardhan's study (1986) is an improvement. However, his definition of poverty in terms of a fixed expenditure level for all regions is not appropriate.

Bardhan also analyses cross-section data for West Bengal in

1977-78 and for 55 NSS regions for 1972-73. In the regional model, he uses natural (geo-physical), infrastructural, demographic, social and economic-institutional variables in explaining poverty. (Bardhan, 1982, 1986). However, his dependent variable is per capita monthly expenditure at 1960-61 prices of non-cultivator wage-earner households.

Bigger household size (Dandekar and Rath, 1971, Gaiha, 1981), higher dependency ratio (Gaiha, 1981), level of illiteracy (Gaiha, 1981), higher percentage of unemployment (Visaria, 1980) and regional characteristics have also been found to be associated with higher poverty.

Ahluwalia concludes from the analysis of the temporal pattern of poverty that there is a strong evidence of an inverse relationship between agricultural income per head and incidence of rural poverty specially if account is taken of lagged effect. Other features influencing poverty mentioned by him are:

(a) Land-man ratio;
(b) Nature of technology;
(c) Progressive enhancing of the capacity of small and marginal farmers;
(d) Factors affecting the rural labour markets;
(e) The state of labour organisations;
(f) The state and nature of rural unemployment programme; and
(g) The state of urban labour markets (Ahluwalia, 1986:73).

Jain postulates relationships of poverty with many socio-economic variables, establishes hypotheses and tests the same for cross-state as well as time-series data. After conducting a preliminary exercise using data given by Ganguli and Gupta (1976:168), Jain develops his own models. (Jain 1987:113-123). The dependent variables are the head-count ratio, poverty-gap, Sen's indicators, Kakwani indicators and Jain's own indicators calculated for 1960-61 and 1970-71 for 15 major states in India. In his cross-state model, he uses 10 explanatory variables which are basically economic in nature. These are: per capita state domestic product (PCSDP), concentration ratio for distribution of assets (CR), Gini coefficient of consumer expenditure distribution (G), Employment rate (UWF) (which is in fact participation rate), share of population (PU), that of the poor (UP), average earnings of all factory workers (AEFW), average number of persons employed in factories (ADEF), Education indicators (EI), and percentage of rural households having land less than one acre (LHH). In his cross-state model, though the fits are goods, most of the explanatory variables have no significant relationship with the poverty measures. In fact, education is the only universally significant indicator and strangely all the poverty measures are positively related with education. Thus, poverty is higher in states with higher level of education.[7] This can be true in the case of rural poverty models in 1960-61. In the 1970-71 model, he does not introduce the education indicator, still the fits are very good. In 1970-71, inequality measures have attained significant importance in explaining poverty. PU, G and LHH explain variance in most of the variants of poverty measures, especially the Head-count measure. Since R^2 is very high and *t*-ratios are low, the problem of multicollinearity is present. Moreover, degrees of freedom are also lost since too many variables have been introduced. He has, therefore, dropped many variables in rural and urban cross-section models for 1960-61. Education and inequality indictors (G) are the most significant variables in rural India and PCSDP and PSSN in urban areas. In the urban areas, the fits are very poor. For 1970-71, as already pointed out, LHH, PU and G are the significant explanatory variables in rural areas and PCSDP, PU and G in urban areas. Universally, H is the best explained poverty indicator in rural and urban areas.

In time-series models, in which 15 explanatory variables are introduced, the results are not quite different. On the basis of these results, especially the time-series results, Jain comes to the conclusion that the major instruments of policy required for the eradication of poverty are as follows:

(1) Employment generation, particularly for the poor unorganised labour.
(2) Increasing the availability of foodgrains and controlling their prices.
(3) Reduction of inequalities in the distribution of income and wealth, and
(4) Ensuring price stability. (Jain, 1987:123).

This study is lacking in some very important aspects. Poverty is a consequence of the operation of a variety of factors. In his listing of the explanatory variables he has mixed the causal variables with the result variables. In fact, he has neglected the study of ultimate factors causing poverty and listed only proximate causes of poverty. Specially, his neglect of geo-physical and infrastructural variables, as also the indicators of agrarian structure is regrettable, and, therefore, in his model the specification errors of exclusion of many relevant variables and inclusion of many irrelevant variables have been committed. This has, naturally, affected his conclusions significantly.

Conclusion

From the perusal of the studies on poverty and its correlates, it is seen that researchers have confused between correlates and causative variables and between proximate and ultimate causes e.g., Bardhan in his analysis takes several heterogeneous variables in the same model. He has, in fact, taken average annual rate of growth of agricultural output as well as the growth generating variables like percentage of area irrigated, use of electric pump-sets and oil engines. However, Rao, Gupta and Sharma considered these factors separately. Jain has also clubbed the development level, growth, infrastructural, institutional and other variables together in the same model.

Attempt is made here to avoid these pit-falls. In the study of correlates of poverty, attention is centered on the key variables which are likely to be directly associated with poverty. The variables influencing these key variables have been studied separately so that appropriate policy conclusions regarding the nature of the key variables can be derived. Moreover, as already pointed out, regression as such is not of much interest. For this type of work, regression analysis and development of composite indicators is not of much help. Clustering techniques and other techniques of development of typology are relevant here.

In each block of variables, first the zero-order correlation matrix between all the indicators is examined. The variables having high correlation with each other and also being conceptually similar are then combined into composite indicators. However, variables not showing high correlation or variables which are conceptually uncorrelated are taken separately. Similarly, if variables in one block are conceptually related with variables in other block, for example, if variables of agricultural output and productivity are related to infrastructural and input variables in another block, then this relationship will also be studied. However, if necessary, the blocks may still be represented by separate variables.

In this way, several individual or composite indicators representing different blocks of variables are obtained and then regression studies are undertaken. Ultimately, introducing significant variables from the block-wise regression, one linear relationship is estimated using step by step ordinary least squares.

II
RURAL POVERTY AND ITS CORRELATES REGRESSION RESULTS FOR REGIONS

Introduction

In this section we analyse the NSS cross-region household consumption and expenditure data in the light of the geo-physical and structural correlates of poverty. We use three indicators of poverty in this analysis:

(i) Percentage of ultra-poor households i.e., rural households failing to obtain a daily calorie norm of 1920. Alternatively, we have taken a composite indicator of the head-count ratio, poverty gap and Sen's indicator (P);
(ii) Average per capita expenditure of rural households (APE); and
(iii) A measure of real per capita income (RY).

It may be noted that Rao et. al. (1986:87) took a calorie norm of 2200 per capita per day and calculated the proportion of rural population failing to achieve this norm. Alternatively, they as well as recently Jain and associates (1988:2395-2408) adopted a monthly expenditure of Rs. 15 at 1960-61 prices adjusted for price changes during this period. Bardhan (1986:87) took two surrogate indicators of poverty: per capita monthly expenditure level of the non-cultivator rural households that were poor in terms of the value of assets. The latter is defined here as asset deprivation. In an earlier study, (Bardhan, 1984, 1986: 196) took per capita monthly expenditure level of non-cultivating wage-earner households as an indicator of poverty of agricultural labour households. However, taking his two non-cultivator wage-earner based indicators as surrogate indicators of overall rural poverty will create errors in measurement, since poverty does exist among other segments/sections of the rural population (Sagar et al, 1987) and there is a no reason to hypothesise a one to one correspondence between the indicators of poverty chosen by Bardhan and an indicator of poverty for the rural population as a whole.

Since asset ownership is one of the most important ultimate inputs in determining the levels of income, expenditure and food intake, we have chosen it as a causative factor rather than as a dependent variable. Bardhan has given no reason for adopting these two indicators as representing overall rural poverty. Hence, we stick to our three surrogate indicators of poverty.

Bardhan in his 1984 study uses a linear regression model and tries several demographic, geophysical, and economic, institutional and technological variables. Similar sets of variables are used in his other study (1986:88-90). Rao and associates also take a set of institutional, infrastructural and technological and productivity variables. They specify a loglinear relationship and run separate regressions for the three sets of causative factors. (Rao et al, 1986: 95-108).

We have grouped the correlates of poverty in the following meaningful categories (full list of indicators is given in appendix to chapter I).

(1) Forces of production in agriculture, including

- (a) Geophysical conditions
- (b) Development of infrastructure
- (c) Use of inputs and capital base; and
- (d) Output and productivity

(2) Land relations including reso ·ce deprivation
(3) Labour relations
(4) Credit relations
(5) Demographic variables
(6) Social oppression and remoteness
(7) Development of manufacturing

We use a linear specification and first run regressions for each group of variables and then re-run the final regressions with only the significant variables taken as regressors.

It may be remembered that the calorie intake according to

expenditure classes in Jammu and Kashmir mountainous is highly irregular. Smoothening of the distribution is almost impossible. Hence the nutrition based poverty and income deprivation indicators have not been computed for this region. Thus, poverty data relate to only 63 regions. Moreover, the data about several variables are unavailable for many regions, mostly for region Nos. 58 to 63. Hence, regressions have been run only for 57 regions. In individual cases, wherever data are not available, the number of regions is even smaller.

Blockwise Regressions Forces of Production in Agriculture

Geophysical Conditions, Infrastructure and Inputs

It can be hypothesised that (a) poverty is lower the higher is average annual rainfall (NR), (b) the smaller is the instability in rainfall (percentage deficit rainfall (DEFRAIN) proportion of annual rainfall concentrated in June-September monsoon, CRAIN)). (c) in regions where soil rating for agricultural purposes is higher (SOIL), poverty is expected to be lower.[8]

Geophysical conditions are rectified and supplemented with the help of infrastructure development. The most important indicator of agricultural infrastructure development is the per cent of sown area irrigated (IRR). However, source and nature of irrigation projects has an important bearing on the distribution of the benefits of irrigation. We have taken two indicators of these aspects: the number of electric pumpsets and oil engines used per hectare of cropped area (EP) and per cent area irrigated by wells and tube wells (IWT).

The impact of irrigation facility on farm activity is reflected in the intensity of cropping (IC). It is expected that (a) irrigation lowers the incidence of poverty, and (b) intensity of cropping also lowers the level of poverty (Rao et al, 1986:98). However, the sign of relationship of poverty with EP and IWT is not unambiguous (Bardhan, 1984: 197).

Use of modern agricultural inputs like fertilizers (FERT), pesticides, high yielding seeds etc., is generally concentrated in irrigated areas. Hence, there will be, in general, high positive correlation between FERT, IRR and EP. Thus, poverty will be lower in states with larger use of fertilizers.

The zero-order correlation coefficients between poverty measure and geophysical and infrastructure variables show that except in the case of NR, signs are as hypothesised but the coefficients are statistically significant at 5 per cent level only for NR and IRR.

There are relatively very large inter-regional differentials in the development of infrastructure. C.V. of variables EP, IRR, IWT, FERT and NR is high. All of these, except NR, are policy instruments. Thus, the policy of infrastructural development has increased inter-regional differentials.

Regressing *P* on all these variables simultaneously, all parameter values except those pertaining to *IRR* and *NR* are statistically insignificant. High rainfall regions are prone to be poor. Dropping all variables with t values of parameter estimates less than 1, we obtain the following results:

$$P = 1.086 + 3.42\ 10^{-5}{*}\ NR - 8.34\ 10^{-4}\ \text{DEFRAIN}$$
$$t = (1.8931) \qquad (-1.0344)$$
$$-4.79\ 10^{-4}\ \text{IWT} - 2.12\ 10^{-3}{*}\ \text{IRR} \quad +.6263{*}\ \text{EP}$$
$$(-1.1159) \qquad (-3.3773) \quad (2.0591)$$
$$R^2 = .3721{*}, F = 5.3341, N = 51$$

* Significant at 5 per cent level.

The five variables explain 37 per cent of the variance in the inter-region differentials in the incidence of poverty. However, only the relationships with *IRR*, *EP* and *NR* are significant. States with high normal rainfall have higher proportion of poor in the rural population (Bardhan, op cit.)

Irrigation reduces poverty, whereas energisation of wells, other things remaining same, raises poverty by, perhaps, distributing benefits in favour of the rich. As against irrigation by canals, irrigation by energised wells is class-biased. (Bardhan, 1984:197).

In order to reduce variable over-weight, we computed a composite indicator of the infrastructure and input variables (EP, IRR, FERT, IWT, & IC). The first principal component explains as much as 44.35 per cent of the variance in these five variables. However, the weights of IWT and IC are quite low. Hence, dropping these two, we have computed the composite infrastructure and input index (CII). The index explains 72.4 per cent of the variance in the component indicators.

Capital Base

Income also depends upon the capital base whether the rural households are engaged in cultivation, animal husbandry or non-agricultural productive activities. Here, we have taken four indicators:

1. Average value of land
2. Average value of total assets
3. Average value of livestock
4. Average value of implements

and calculated a composite indicator of capital base (or resource base) of RHH (CIA). This indicator explains 77.8 per cent of the variance in the included variables.

Regressing P on NR, DEFRAIN, CRAIN, SOILR, composite indicator of capital base (CIA) and composite indicator of infrastructural development and input use (CII), we get the following fit:

$$
\begin{aligned}
P = {} & 0.8724 + \underset{(1.0689)}{1.77\,10^{-5}\,\text{NR}} + \underset{(2.1446)}{9.65\,10^{-4}{}^{*}\,\text{DEFRAIN}} \\
& \underset{(-.5948)}{-4.25\,10^{-4}\,\text{CRAIN}} \underset{(-.0690)}{-8.74\,10^{-5}\,\text{SOILR}} \underset{(-4.4275)}{-.0871^{*}\,\text{CIA}} + \underset{(.7754)}{.0128\,\text{CII}} \\
& R^2 = 0.4806^{*}, F = 6.784, d.f.\ (6,44)
\end{aligned}
$$

As expected, the most important effect on poverty in regions is the capital base. In fact, it overshadows the effect of the development of infrastructure and rainfall. Raising infrastructure, keeping asset base unchanged, will not reduce poverty. Keeping other variables unchanged, instability in rainfall raises poverty. The results are confirmed by the poverty model of states for the early eighties. (Mehta, 1990).

Hence, raising the capital base of the rural households and reducing instability in agriculture caused by instability in rainfall are the main policy variables in the programme for poverty eradication.

As already discussed, Bardhan and many other researchers have taken per capita household expenditure as an alternative measure of poverty. These variables are negatively inter-correlated. We have taken two measures of average per capita expenditure, one in nominal terms given by the NSS (APE) and the other in real terms or, more precisely, colorie equivalent expenditure or income (RY). Real income indicator is defined here as the ratio of APE to the ultrapoverty line expenditure. There are large inter-region variations in APE and RY, coefficient of variation (C.V.) is 22.9 and 37.8 per cent, respectively.

The regression results for these measures of poverty are[9]:

$$\begin{aligned} APE = \text{constant} &+ 9.39\ 10^{-4}\ NR - .0790\ DEFRAIN + .0918\ CRAIN \\ &\quad (.5966) \qquad (-1.6688) \qquad (1.3504) \\ &- .02873\ SOILR + 13.4392^{*}\ CIA + 3.1197^{*}\ CII \\ &\quad (-.2367) \qquad (7.1887) \qquad (1.9802) \end{aligned}$$

$R^2 = 0.7134^{*}, \bar{R}^2 = 0.6743 \quad F = 18.25, d.f.\ (6,44)$

$$\begin{aligned} RY = &-1.04\ 10^{-4}\ NR - 9.66\ (10)^{-3*}\ DEFRAIN + 4.19\ 10^{-3}\ CRAIN \\ &\quad (-1.0615) \qquad (-3.6049) \qquad (.9910) \\ &+ .0002\ SOILR + .6244^{*}\ CIA + .0200\ CII \\ &\quad (.0210) \qquad (5.3704) \qquad (.2039) \end{aligned}$$

$R^2 = 0.6146^{*}, \bar{R}^2 = 0.5620, F = 11.694, d.f. = 6,44$

The fits are better but are basically similar to that for poverty (P).

Agricultural Output, Productivity and Instability

Poverty can generally be expected to be lower in regions with higher agricultural yield per hectare and per capita as well as higher growth rate (Ahluwalia, 1978, 1986, Bardhan, 1982 and Saith, 1981, Srinivasan and Bardhan, 1974). However, the benefits might not accrue to the rural poor if the increased agricultural productivity is obtained by labour saving devices or by displacing marginal and small farmers (Bardhan, 1982, 1986). Hence the relationship between poverty and per hectare yield is open ended (Mundle, 1983, Griffin and Ghosh, 1979), while that with output per capita is expected to be negative.

Regressing P on OPC and OPH[10], we obtain the following results.

$$\begin{aligned} P = 1.0151 &- 2.89\ 10^{-4*}OPC + 7.15\ 10^{-5*}\ OPH \\ &\quad (-4.3245) \qquad (2.8605) \end{aligned}$$

$R^2 = 0.2990^{*}, F = 11.3048, d.f. = (2,52), n = 56$

The hypotheses are supported by our results. Thus poverty cannot be eliminated only by raising per hectare yields. This might also be because of population pressure. However, the two variables are insufficient to explain the inter-region variations in poverty. It should be noted that the correlation between OPC and OPH is not high (r=.2103). Thus, raising per hectare yields does not *ipso facto* raise per capita or per worker output. There has been no appreciable change in the relationship in early eighties as revealed by cross-state data (Mehta, 1990).

It should be remembered that output is only an intermediate factor influencing poverty. Output level depends upon many factors. Regressing output per capita (OPC) and output per hectare (OPH) on variables representing geophysical, infrastructural and capital base conditions we obtain the following results.

$$\begin{aligned} OPC = {} & \text{Constant} + .0258\ NR - 2.0144^{*}\ CRAIN + 2.0426\ SOILR \\ & \qquad (1.1571) \quad (-2.0963) \qquad (1.1897) \\ & - 0.2351\ DEFRAIN + 228.681^{*}\ CIA + 27.1906\ CII \\ & (-.3859) \qquad (8.6511) \qquad (1.2206) \end{aligned}$$

$$R^2 = 0.7633^{*}, \bar{R}^{2} = 0.7311, F = 23.6542, n = 51, d.f. = (6,44)$$

$$\begin{aligned} OPH = {} & \text{Constant} + .3266^{*}NR - 4.4691\ CRAIN + 6.1795\ SOILR \\ & \qquad (5.1058) \quad (-1.6206) \qquad (1.2542) \\ & 0.5269\ DEFRAIN + 1.0878\ CIA + 394.6580^{*}CII \\ & (.3014) \qquad (.0143) \qquad (6.1733) \end{aligned}$$

$$R^2 = 0.7265^{*}, \bar{R}^{2} = 0.6892, F = 19.4781, d.f. = 6,44$$

Only two factors CRAIN and Capital base (CIA) explain most of the variance in OPC. Similarly, only two factors NR and CII explain the variance in OPH. Hence, in the place of the rainfall and capital base and infrastructure variables, we can consider the two output variables OPC and OPH or vice versa.

Taking the other poverty measures, APE and RY, we see that the regression results are better (R^2 is higher). Only OPC is the significant variable explaining inter-regional disparity in average nominal per capita expenditure and real per capita expenditure.

$$\begin{aligned} APE = {} & \text{Constant} + .0418^{*}\ OPC - 1.0895\ 10^{-3*}\ OPH \\ & \qquad (6.2317) \qquad (-.4352) \end{aligned}$$

$$R^2 = 0.4328^{*}, \quad n = 55$$

$$RY = \text{Constant} + 2.0356\ 10^{-3} * OPC - 2.7837\ 10^{-4}\ OPH$$
$$(4.8901) \qquad (-1.7909)$$
$$R^2 = 0.3205^*, \quad n = 55$$

Land and Resource Deprivation and Land Relations

Resource Deprivation

Other things remaining same, poverty is expected to be high in regions in which a large proportion of rural people are deprived of physical and human resources, the most important being the deprivation of land and implements. As already explained, we have taken three indicators of resource deprivation:

AD : Index of asset deprivation — per cent of households owning assets worth less than Rs. 2500

LD : Composite land deprivation index being composed of per cent of households owning land less than 2.5 acres and pressure on land.

COLA : Composite index of concentration of land and assets. (See chapter 3 for details)

There are no sharp inter-regional variations in these variables, C.V. is less than 10 per cent. As expected, all the three are positively inter-correlated. However, the relationship is not very strong ($r = \leq 0.76$). All these variables raise poverty. Correlation coefficients of P with AD, LD and COLA are 0.66, 0.44 and 0.43, respectively. They are with proper signs and are statistically significant at 5 per cent level.

Results of running multivariate regression are given in table 5.1. It is found that the fit is good, R^2 being 0.4592 and F=15.29, the coefficient for COLA is statistically not significant and its sign is also perverse. Dropping this variable does not affect the fit, evidently COLA is dominated by AD and LD. Index of asset deprivation is enough to explain the interregional differentials in nutritional poverty.[11] However, real income is better explained by the composite index of land deprivation. Real income is low in regions with larger sections of people suffering from land deprivation.

TABLE 5.1: Resource Deprivation and Poverty : Regression Results

Variable	Poverty				APE		RY	
	β	t	β	t	β	t	β	t
AD	0.0586*	4.5212	.0533*	5.1199	1.3593*	.8923	−.0182	−.23
LD	0.0178	1.5965	.0163	1.4988	−5.3539*	−3.644	−.356*	−4.64
COLA	-9.92×10^{-3}	−.6951	—	—	—	—	—	
R^2		.4592		.4543		.2093		.3497
F		15.2864		22.8939		7.0142		14.2484

Leasing Activity

As already pointed out, leasing activities may ease the situation created by the land and asset deprivation. However, the actual relationship depends on the classes to which the leaser and leasee belong and the conditions of leasing. Five indicators of leasing-in and five of leasing-out and one for absentee landlordism are considered. The list can be seen in the appendix to Chapter I.

The zero-order correlation coefficients and their hypothesised signs are given in Table 5.2.

Taken individually, most of the indicators on leasing activity are not correlated with poverty. Only PLOMSF has significant negative effect on interstate poverty profile. This supports our hypothesis.

TABLE 5.2: Poverty and Leasing : Zero-order Correlation Coefficient

		(A) Leasing-out				
Variable	PLO	PLOUM	PLOMF	PLOMSF	PLORF	PALL
Expected Sign	OPEN	+	+	—	—	+
r	−.22	−.08	−.25	−.32*	.13	−.04

		(B) Leasing-in			
Variable	PLI	PLISC	PLIMF	PLISF	PLIMSF
Expected Sign	+	+	+	+	+
r	−.08	−.22	.11	−.21	.007

Multiple regression results show poor fits ($R^2 = 0.28$ and $F = 1.6647$) and only two parameter estimates, those for PLO and PLOMSF are statistically significant. Both are negative. However, signs of most of the other coefficients are in accordance with the hypotheses. (Table 5.3).

Labour Market Relations

Poverty is positively correlated with the percentage of wage labour in the total labour force, specially the percentage of casual workers (Visaria, 1980:27, 31, 32) and percentage of agricultural labourers (Dandekar and Rath, 1971) and negatively correlated with agricultural productivity and wage income per agricultural worker (Visaria, 1980:27-32).[12]

TABLE 5.3: Land Relations and Poverty : Regression Results

Variable	β	t
PLO	−0.0153*	−2.2569
PLOUM	.0151	1.3058
PLOMF	2.4×10^{-3}	0.8081
PLORF	1.63×10^{-4}	1.2806
PLOMSF	-3.72×10^{-3}*	−2.2371
PALL	1.22×10^{-3}	1.0281
PLI	3.23×10^{-3}	1.4548
PLISC	1.08×10^{-3}	0.3856
PLIMF	4.45×10^{-3}	1.0559
PLISF	-3.54×10^{-3}	−1.3600
PLIMSF	7.63×10^{-4}	0.3380

$R^2 = 0.28, F = 1.6647$

The proportion of agricultural labourer households in the total farm population is expected to be higher the greater is the development of capitalist relations in agriculture. Therefore, poverty ought to be lower in regions with higher proportion of agricultural labourer households in comparison to regions in which feudal or semi-feudal relations are still dominant. However, in initial stages, the higher proportion of agricultural labourer households may indicate concealed tenancy and/or increased pauperisation of the rural masses. Hence, the sign of the relationship cannot be hypothesised, specially when agricultural labourers are working as casual workers.

Following variables have been taken to represent the operation of the labour market:

AgL/Cul	=	Ratio of agricultural labourers to cultivators.
RFL	=	Regular farm labour as proportion of total male farm labour in age-group of 15-55 years (100 — % of casual labour force, CL).
WL	=	Proportion of farm wage labour in rural labour force in the age group of 15-59 years.

These variables represent the supply and composition of labour in rural market. The demand situation as well as interaction of demand and supply is reflected by the following variables:

URR = Average daily rural unemployment rate.

AWE = Average rate of earnings per man day of farm wage work for males in the age-group of 15-55 years in rural non-cultivator wage earning households in 1970-71.

LABPROD = Labour productivity in triennium ending 1964-65.

Poverty is expected to be negatively correlated with AWE, LABPROD and RFL and positively with the other supply side variable and unemployment rate. Zero-order correlation coefficients between these variables show that, as expected, unemployment and proportion of wage workers, specially that of the casual workers, raise poverty, higher average wage earnings and labour productivity reduces poverty but the results are statistically not significant.

The best multiple regression results are reported below:

$$P = \text{Constant} + 5.024\ 10^{-3}{*}\text{URR} + 3.5078\ 10^{-3}{*}\ \text{WL}$$
$$(2.8352) \qquad (2.8856)$$
$$-9.0768\ 10^{-4}\ \text{AgL/Cul} - .0014{*}\ \text{RFL} - .0287\ \text{LABPROD}$$
$$(-1.3727) \qquad (-2.7587) \qquad (-1.0878)$$
$$R^2 = 0.6080{*}, \bar{R}^2 = 0.5688, F = 15.5087$$

$$APE = \text{Constant} + .1984\ \text{URR} - .5016{*}\text{WL} + .2437{*}\text{AgL/Cul}$$
$$(.9461) \qquad (-3.5229) \qquad (3.1057)$$
$$+ .0685\ \text{RFL} + 13.2868{*}\ \text{LABPROD}$$
$$(1.155) \qquad (4.2163)$$
$$R^2 = 0.5583,\ \bar{R}^2 = 0.5132,\ F = 12.3854$$

$$RY = \text{Constant} - 7.7909\ 10^{-3}\ \text{UR} - .0269{*}\ \text{WL}$$
$$(-.6208) \qquad (-3.1306)$$
$$+ .0103{*}\text{AgL/Cul} + 8.9266\ 10^{-3}{*}\ \text{RFL} + .3769{*}\ \text{LABPROD}$$
$$(2.1850) \qquad (2.5144) \qquad (1.9981)$$
$$R^2 = 0.5139{*}, \bar{R}^2 = 0.4643, F = 10.3605$$

Relatively very good fits are obtained. 60.80 per cent of the inter-region differentials in poverty are explained by the five labour market variables and the signs are as hypothesised. The ambiguity about the role of agricultural labourers is revealed by the negative sign, though the coefficient is statistically not significant at 10 per cent level of significance. Unemployment rate, proportion of wage workers to the labour force and the predominance of the casual workers all increase poverty. In contrast, the poverty reducing role of productivity and wage earnings is also confirmed.[13]

Real income is higher in regions providing regular employment at higher wage earnings and also where capitalist relations are more developed (high AgL/Cul). However, unemployment has no effect. Similar results are obtained for APE. Productivity and class variables are the most significant ones, perhaps due to common trend. Since income influences all explanatory variables taken here, the problem of reverse causation exists. There is simultaneity bias in the results obtained.

Rural Debt and Credit Relations

Credit market conditions in combination with landownership and leasing and labour market conditions are expected to have profound effect on the poverty scenario. On the basis of the discussion of the relationships in Section I of this chapter and Section II of the next chapter, it can be hypothesised that high percentage of households indebted (PIND) but low average debt (ADEBT), taken primarily for consumption purposes (DCP and PDHH), mainly from the professional moneylenders and traders (DPMLT) and, in some situations, from agricultural moneylenders (DAgML), on usufructuary mortgage (PLOUM) would lead to a high debt-asset ratio (DAR) and high poverty. On the other hand, high or average credit taken from institutional agencies (DIA) and/or from agricultural moneylenders (DAgML), on other than usufructuary mortgage and at a reasonable rate of interest, primarily for farm or non-farm business (DFB, DNFB), is expected to be reflected in low debt-asset ratio (DAR) and low poverty. Hence, the signs of the zero-order correlation coefficients are likely to be misleading.

Several indicators are considered to represent the working of the credit market. These are:

> ADEBT, PIND, PDHH, DCP, DFB, DAR, DIA, DAgML, DPMLT. The variables pertain to cash dues outstanding for all rural households.

The relationship between poverty and credit market indicators is quite weak, perhaps, because of the possibility of the different forms of agrarian relations pulling the relationship in opposing directions.

TABLE 5.4: Zero-order Correlation Matrix: Credit Market: All Rural Households

	P	PDHH	DCP	DIA	DLL	DAgML	DPMLT	DFB	DAR	ADEBT	PIND	
POVERTY	1											
PDHH	−.32*	1										
DCP	−.23	.41*	1									
DIA	−.30*	.48*	.77*	1								
DLL	+.01	.06	.09	.28		1						
DAgML	−.14	.23	.34*	.49*		.59*	1					
DPMLT	−.46*	.50*	.44*	.50*		−.30*	−.10	1				
DFB	−.26	.18	.74*	.68*		.19	.31	.25	1			
DAR	+.08	.57*	−.14	.08		.17	.23	.06	−.29*	1		
ADEBT	−.33*	.48*	−.23	−.09		.08	.08	.08	−.28*	.67*	1	
PIND	−.27*	.87*	.05	.12		.03	.11	.34*	−.18	.69*	.70*	1
MEAN		27.3	41.4	68.6		6.7	18.2	23.5	52.8	.05	539.6	42.0
C.V.		36.3	34.1	26.4		90.7	68.1	54.4	30.9	55.3	59.6	27.6

All the statistically significant zero-order correlation coefficients between poverty and credit market variables are negative (Table 5.4). A hypothesis can therefore, be advanced that in poor regions credit availability for all purposes and from different sources is low. Dues outstanding should, perhaps, be taken as an indicator of credit availability and not as a burden. However, nothing certain can be asserted in this regard because of reverse causation and the operation of other factors.

Regressing poverty on all these variables together, we find that the coefficients of DAR, ADEBT and DPMLT are statistically significant (Table 5.5).

TABLE 5.5: Poverty and Credit Market: Multivariate Linear Regression Results

Explanatory Variable	Regression Coefficient	t-Value
PDHH	$1.11X10^{-3}$	0.3219
DCP	$1.04X10^{-3}$	0.8171
DIA	$-7.49X10^{-4}$	−0.6321
DLL	$3.58X10^{-4}$	0.1716
DAgML	$-1.83X10^{-3}$	−1.6989
DPMLT	$-3.03X10^{-3}$*	−2.6920
DFB	$-8.14X10^{-4}$	−0.8246
DAR	2.30*	3.9870
ADEBT	$-1.86X10^{-4}$*	−3.9448
PIND	$-1.75X10^{-3}$	−0.5903
CONSTANT	1.1845	

$R^2 = 0.5557^*$, $\bar{R}^2 = 0.4594$, $F = 5.7541$

Thus, larger the credit availability, lower the poverty. However, large debt in relation to assets (DAR) may indicate distress borrowing, hence it raises poverty. If credit is available for productive purposes then source does not matter. Signs of coefficients of DPMLT & DAgML are all negative. Signs of PDHH and DCP are proper but the coefficients are statistically not significant. A glance at the zero-order correlation matrix reveals that the problem of multicollinearity is not serious in the regression, only PIND and PDHH have relatively high coefficient of correlation ($r=.87$).

Dropping variables with absolute value of t-ratio less than unity and reregressing poverty on DAgML, DPMLT, DAR and ADEBT, we obtain the following result:

$$P = \text{Constant} - .0022^{*}\text{DAgML} - 3.4853\ 10^{-4*}\ \text{DPMLT}$$
$$-(2.9247) \qquad (-5.0023)$$
$$+ 2.2307^{*}\text{DAR} \quad -2.0345\ 10^{-4*}\text{ADEBT}$$
$$(4.8530) \qquad (-5.4684)$$
$$R^2 = 0.5355^{*}, \bar{R}^{2} = 0.4988, F = 14.9876$$

The results are substantially improved. All t-values, $\bar{R}^{2}$ and F ratios have improved markedly. The results already stated are confirmed. To repeat, large credit availability reduces poverty even when the source is agricultural moneylenders or professional moneylenders. However, larger credit in the absence of proper asset base (high DAR) becomes burden and, therefore, raises poverty.[14]

If we measure poverty by low nominal and real expenditure (income) then the following results are obtained:

$$\text{APE} = \text{Constant} + 0.299\ \text{PDHH} + 0.0173\ \text{DCP}$$
$$(1.0977) \qquad (0.1802)$$
$$-312.382^{*}\ \text{DAR} + 0.0357^{*}\text{ADEBT} - 0.1363\ \text{PIND}$$
$$(-6.2555) \qquad (8.0916) \qquad (-0.5854)$$

$$R^2 = 0.6574^{*}, \bar{R}^2 = 0.6232, F = 19.1925, n = 56$$

$$\text{RY} = \text{Constant} + 0.0230\ \text{PDHH} + 3.3614\ 10^{-3}\ \text{DCP}$$
$$(1.4198) \qquad (0.5871)$$
$$-19.048\ \text{DAR}^{*} + 1.2880\ 10^{-3*}\text{ADEBT} + 6.3427\ 10^{-3}\text{PIND}$$
$$(-6.4048) \qquad (4.9028) \qquad (0.4574)$$

$$R^2 = 0.5880^{*}, \bar{R}^2 = 0.5468, F = 14.2747$$

Both nominal and real expenditure are high and, therefore, poverty low in regions in which average credit available is larger and debt asset ratio (DAR) is low.

When we regress APE on the indicators of the source of finance, we find that no indicator is statistically significant at even 10 per cent level of significance. However, following results are obtained for real expenditure (RY):

$$\begin{aligned} RY = \text{Constant} &+ 0.0134^{**}DIA + 0.0202\,DLL \\ &\quad (1.7800) \qquad\quad (1.3605) \\ &+ 8.0094\,10^{-3}\,DAgML + 0.0304^{*}\,DPMLT \\ &\quad (1.0131) \qquad\quad (3.8737) \\ &- 0.0088\,DFB \\ &\quad (-1.4281) \end{aligned}$$

$R^2 = 0.2824^*, \bar{R}^2 = 0.2107, F = 3.9357$

** Significant at 5 per cent level for one-tailed test.

Hence, in regions where larger credit is available from institutional agencies, real income is high and poverty is low. Similar remarks apply for credit available from professional moneylenders and traders.

Since credit from institutional agencies DIA= (100-DNIA) and debt for farm and non-farm business(DFB) are positively intercorrelated and PDHH, DAR, ADEBT and PIND are highly intercorrelated (Table 5.4), we have prepared the composite indicators DCI_1 and DCI_2 from these two sets and regressed poverty, APE and RY on these composite indicators alongwith all the remaining variables of credit market. The results are relatively very poor when compared to those already reported. Only the variable credit provided by professional moneylenders and traders (DPMLT) shows significant relationship with real income and poverty and only DCI_2 with APE. Hence, the results reported earlier are retained.

All the above results are based on the distribution of total debt by source and purpose. This may be misleading for poverty studies. A small number of rich farmers may take large proportion of loans. The percentage distribution of total debt of all rural households will closely follow the distribution of debt of these better-off households. This distribution will fail to reflect the true position of the majority of rural households. Therefore, the relationship of the percentage of rural households reporting taking loans from various agencies with the poverty measures has also been studied. The results are similar to those already obtained, though R^2 is lowered. Hence, in this study, percentage distribution of debt by source (agency) can be taken to represent percentage distribution of households reporting loans from the credit agencies.

To see whether debt by purpose and source taken by agricultural labourers in particular causes poverty, *P* is regressed on the variables PDHH, DCP, DNIA, DLL, AgML, DPML, DT related to agricultural labourers. The fit is very poor, R^2=0.2315, which is statistically not significant at 5 per cent level, only the signs of regression coefficients of DCP and DT are positive. However, no coefficient is statistically significant at 5 per cent level.

Demographic Variables

Gender-Bias, Population Pressure, Mortality and Poverty

Because of gender-bias in employment, wages and nutrition, poverty is expected to be higher in states with higher sex-ratio (SR, Females per 1000 males) (Agarwal, 1986:189, Parthasarathy 1982, and Visaria and Visaria, 1983). In the absence of reliable data about female headedness (FH) and female and male mortality rates for all regions, sex ratio is taken as a proxy for gender-bias. In the state level study, it was found that the poverty index is positively correlated with FH and negatively with female/male mortality rate ratio both in the early seventies and the early eighties. (Mehta, 1990:61-63) Thus, the hypothesis about the relationship between poverty and SR is confirmed.

Population pressure is reflected by population density (PD), Physiological density (PhyD) and rate of population growth. Regions with population pressure are expected to show larger proportion of the poor. Death rate is an important demographic variable. Survival ratio (SURR) is taken as the variable representing reverse of mortality. Poverty is expected to be lower in regions in which survival ratio is high.

The correlation coefficients of poverty with only PD (0.31), SR (0.50) and PhyD (0.17) are statistically significant and the signs are also as hypothesised. Though the two density measures are expected to move in the same direction yet, because of large uncultivated or hilly tracts in some regions, the two are not correlated very closely (r=.48). the other measure of population pressure, (gp), is not related to density at all (r=0.09). Thus, the static and dynamic aspects of population pressure are not related to each other. As hypothesised, sex ratio is positively correlated with poverty (r=0.50) and negatively, but not significantly, with the survival ratio (r=-0.07).[15]

Results of regressing poverty indicator on the demographic indicators are given in Table 5.6.

TABLE 5.6: Poverty and Demographic Variables : Regression Results

Indicator	P		APE		RY	
	β	t	β	t	β	t
PD	$2.55X10^{-4}$*	2.5116	$7.13X10^{-3}$	.0576	$-5.38X10^{-4}$	−0.8451
SR	7.00X10 *	4.7501	−0.0729*	−4.0537	$-4.85X10^{-3}$*	−5.2380
gp	$4.15X10^{-4}$	1.2087	−0.0739	−1.7650	$-2.79X10^{-3}$	−1.2973
PhyD	$-9.53X10^{-4}$	−0.1496	−1.4260	−1.8335	−0.0345	−0.8627
SURR	−0.1835	−1.5845	14.9615	1.0585	1.5004*	2.0631
R^2	0.3964*		0.3379*		0.4067*	
F	6.4361		5.0012		6.7191	

In all the three models, sex-bias in poverty is established beyond doubt. The static population pressure measure PD is associated with high poverty in the regions. PhyD is not significant in the presence of PD. However, though the dynamic measure, gp, has appropriate sign in all the three regressions, it is statistically not highly significant. Similarly, the sign of the coefficient of survival ratio is as hypothesised and regions with higher survival chances have lower nutritional poverty and higher real income. The last result points towards the hazards of single equation regressions. Clearly, survival chances depend, besides other factors, on the level of income and nutrition. Similar remarks apply to population growth rate. These results are, thus, tentative and subject to simultaneity bias.

Settlement Pattern and Poverty

Human settlement patterns may be hypothesised to affect the prevalence of poverty. Smaller and scattered villages are handicapped with respect to the provision of essential infrastructure and even of consumer goods and services; local employment and wage rate may also be depressed. (Bardhan, 1984:193). Thus, small and scattered villages are expected to show up with larger poverty. However, the result may be otherwise, if the scattered villages are large or if the small villages are situated near each other. The three variables considered for depicting the size and spacing of villages are: PSV, ASV and ASPACE.[16]

High urbanisation (DU) may relieve pressure for employment,

from agriculture it will increase demand for agricultural production and raise mobility and consciousness. Hence, poverty ought to be lower in regions with high urbanisation. (Bardhan, 1984:193).

The zero-order correlation coefficients of poverty with these four population settlement variables are given in Table 5.7. Positive value of r between ASPACE and ASV (r=0.49) and the negative value of r between ASPACE and PSV (r=-0.25) indicate that large villages are mostly dispersed widely and small villages are clustered near each other. It is for this reason that larger villages show higher poverty.

TABLE 5.7: Poverty and Population Settlement : Zero-order Correlation

Variables	P	DU	PSV	ASPACE	ASV
P	1				
DU	.13	1			
PSV	−.22	−0.44*	1		
ASPACE	.09	−0.01	−0.25	1	
ASV	.44*	0.02	−0.37*	0.49*	1
MEAN		18.5	21.7	2.7	1289.0
C.V.		56.4	75.4	45.4	1896.2

There are very large inter-regional variation in population settlement pattern in India as evidenced by the coefficient of variation. This is also confirmed by our multivariate regression results (Table 5.8).

Controlling for spacing of villages, bigger average village size has adverse effect on real income and it raises poverty. Other variables have nearly no effect.

TABLE 5.8: Poverty and Population Settlement: Regression Results

Variable	Poverty		APE		RY	
	β	t	β	t	β	t
DU	9.34×10^{-4}	0.778	1.0745	0.4787	3.9×10^{-3}	−.475
PSV	-1.70×10^{-4}	−0.204	−0.0443	0.412	-1.89×10^{-3}	−.334
ASPACE	−0.0122	−1.173	0.3009	0.223	0.0108	.153
ASV	1.91×10^{-4}*	3.475	-2.13×10^{-4}	−0.301	-7.15×10^{-5}**	−1.913
R^2		0.228*		.016		.082
F		3.921		0.217		1.155

** Significant in one tailed test.

At the state level, the signs are similar, except that of PSV which turns out to be positive, though statistically not significant at even 10 per cent level, both in the early seventies and early eighties. (Mehta, 1990 : 61-62) Hence, in the absence of statistical significance, the signs and values of the coefficients do not give reliable indication of the relationships, this way or that way.

Social Oppression and Remoteness and Poverty

States with high proportion of socially oppressed classes represented by scheduled castes can be hypothesised to have larger poverty. Simultaneously, tribal people living in remote areas have traditional living pattern, they lack infrastructure facilities and, therefore, are usually among the poorest groups in rural areas. (Subrahmanyan, 1982:65; Bardhan, 1984: 194).

As expected, the distribution of scheduled tribes in regions is highly uneven, some regions having very high proportion and many having very low proportion, the C.V. is as high as 132.2 per cent. Scheduled castes are also highly concentrated in some regions, though the C.V. is much below that for Scheduled Tribes.

According to the zero-order correlation coefficients, though regions with higher proportion of tribal population have larger poverty (r=.25), the hypothesis that regions with large population of scheduled castes ought to have high poverty is not supported by our data (r=-.30). Combining the two variables also does not improve the results (r=.18) although the sign is correct. This is also supported by our inter-state regression results for early seventies as well as early eighties (Mehta, 1990:60). This is in contrast to the results obtained by Bardhan (1984:174).

Results for the other measures of poverty (APE, RY) are also equally poor. Multiple regression exercise confirms the above results (Table 5.9).

Miscellaneous Factors

We have considered three more indicators in the complete models of poverty. These are:

(1) DR: Dependency Ratio
(2) NONAG: Proportion of working population in the region in

manufacturing, repairing and services.

(5) AGR: (Agricultural growth rate) Rate of growth in agricultural production in the region.

TABLE 5.9: Social Oppression and Poverty

Indicator		Poverty	APE		RY	
SC	β	$-2.80X10^{-3}$	0.1882	—	0.0243*	—
	t	(-1.73022)	(1.0093)		(2.4889)	
ST	β	$9.41X10^{-4}$	−0.1693	—	$-5.92X10^{-4}$	—
	t	(1.0962)	(-1.7177)		(-1.1475)	
SCST	β		—	−.1367	—	$-3.20X10^{-3}$
	t			(-1.360)		(-.5763)
R^2		.1099*	.1037	.0325	.1748*	.0006
F		3.3325	3.1252	1.8495	5.7205	.3321

Though, DR is a demographic variable, it cannot be easily classified into the four sub-categories of demographic variables. It is expected that a region showing higher dependency ratio will also have relatively high poverty.

Rate of growth of agricultural output during 1962-65 to 1970-73 is taken to capture the dynamism of the agrarian economy. A poverty ridden economy may attain relatively high rate of growth of agricultural output and, if the trickle-down hypothesis operates, in time to come it will be able to overcome the poverty problems. Even if the trickle-down hypothesis does not work, it will be in a better position to do so in comparison to a stagnant agrarian economy. Hence, this variable is expected to be negatively correlated with poverty.

If the economy of a region is diversified then there is every likelihood of a reduced pressure on land and, therefore the poverty problem is expected to be relatively less acute. (Bardhan, 1984: 197).

However, the indicator chosen to represent diversification of economy is related to employment in the non-agricultural sector and not to value-added in these sectors. Moreover, the variable includes those engaged in village and unorganised manufacturing and service sectors too. These workers often form the poorest strata in rural areas. This indicator may give a misleading measurement of industrialisation. There is thus, likelihood of committing the error in measurement of variable of unknown magnitude and direction.

Hence, the hypothesis regarding sign of the relationship of poverty with NONAG is open-ended.

Regressing the composite index of indicator of poverty (CIP or P), ultrapoverty (PUP), average per capita nominal expenditure (APE) and real income (RY) on the three indicators gives the following results. (Table 5.10).

TABLE 5.10: Miscellaneous Indicators and Poverty : Regression Results

Variable	PUP		CIP		APE		RY	
	β	t	β	t	β	t	β	t
DR	−0.860*	−1.872	−.117	−1.687	.549*	2.52	−.096	−.257
AGR	−0.197*	−5.286	−0.30*	−5.284	.065*	3.692	.0816*	2.635
NOGAG	0.327*	2.918	.053*	3.147	.077	1.454	−.001	−.013
R^2		0.463*		0.467*		0.294*		.121
$\bar{R}^2$		0.431		.436		.252		.070
F		14.64		14.93		7.08		2.35

The three variables are not at all mutually correlated. Best results are obtained with the composite indicator of poverty, R^2 being as high as .467. R^2 with APE and RY is only .294 and .121, respectively.

The variable AGR, is highly significant in all the three regressions and the signs are also as hypothesised. Thus, regions achieving high agricultural growth have lower poverty and higher nominal and real per capita income.[17]

However, the signs of DR and NONAG are not in accordance with the hypothesis. Regions having high dependency ratio exhibit lower poverty though the relationship is statistically not significant at 5 per cent level. Similarly, regions with high DR have high per capita nominal expenditure. This result is very difficult to explain. A tentative explanation may be that the states having lower poverty are in the initial stage of demographic transition and are, therefore, experiencing high population growth and, therefore, high DR. Thus, it may be two-way relationship and applying OLS is likely to produce specification bias.

Regions with higher proportion of labour-force in manufacturing and services exhibit high poverty. Though the sign of relationship between NONAG and APE is as expected the relationship is statistically not significant. NONAG has no relationship whatsoever with the real income indicator. This result implies that industrialisation is as yet too weak to exert substantial effect on the poverty situation.

Results from the Complete Model

A glance at the results obtained in the preceding paragraphs reveals that, after the process of elimination, the following indicators can be retained as significant variables explaining poverty in the regions of India:

I (a) DEFRAIN, (b) CIA, (c) IRR (d) NR (e) FERT (f) DP
II (a) AD, (b) LD, (c) POL
III (a) DPMLT, (b) DAR, (c) DAgML, (d) ADEBT
IV (a) URR, (b) WL, (c) RFL, (d) AgL/CUL, (e) LABPROD
V (a) SC & ST, (b) SR, (c) ASV, (d) SRR
VI (a) AGR, (b) DR, (c) NONAG
VII (a) OPH, (b) OPC
VIII (a) PLO, (b) PLOMSF

In addition to regressing the composite indicator of poverty (CIP), the average per capita expenditure (APE) and real income (RY) on the set of above variables we have also regressed the per cent of ultrapoor (PUP) on the set of variables so that we can test the sensitivity of the results to the definition of poverty. As already noted earlier, the composite indicator of poverty has been derived from the percentage of the ultrapoor (PUP), the poverty gap and Sen's index.

However, income, poverty and agricultural productivity all depend on geographic, socio-cultural, infrastructural and class related variables. Hence, it would be useful to fit the poverty equation in reduced form, i.e., PUP, CIP as well as APE and RY are regressed only on the vector of exogenous variables. In all, 28 variables are included in the exercise. All endogenous variables e.g., APE, RY, SRR, FLIT, OPC, OPH, LABPROD and LR have been excluded from the set of explanatory variables. Unemployment rate is retained since it has been found that variations in it are not explained to any significant level by the set of other explanatory variables. The results of step by step regression are given in Eq. 5.1 to 5.4 in Table 5.11.

TABLE 5.11: Results from the Complete Model

Eq. No. →	5.1		5.2		5.3		5.4	
Dependent Variable →	PUP		CIP		APE		RY	
Exp. Variable	β	Prob	β	Prob	β	Prob	β	Prob
FERT	−.334	.000	−.020	.013	–	–	.158	.004
DEFRAIN	–	–	–	–	–	–	−.267	.088
IRR	.219	.022	–	–	–	–	−.111	.094
AD	.138	.315	.040	.057	–	–	–	–
POL	–	–	−.025	.035	–	–	.181	.091
LD	–	–	–	–	–	–	.481	.016
CIA	−.242	.017	−.035	.014	–	–	.164	.072
SR	.867	.094	.076	.265	−.359	.070	−.718	.039
ASV	.146	.000	.022	.000	–	–	−.032	.111
WL	.317	.012	.056	.002	−.146	.002	−.114	.151
PLOMSF	−.192	.013	−.019	.035	.081	.009	.206	.000
DAgML	−.245	.001	−.021	.023	.034	.232	–	–
DPMLT	−.286	.005	−.036	.014	–	–	.186	.009
DAR	.232	.008	–	–	.181	.001	−.103	.128
ADEBT	–	–	–	–	.238	.000	–	–
SCST	.264	.001	.034	.002	–	–	−.111	.034
NONAG	.218	.009	.035	.003	–	–	−.080	.179
DR	–	–	−.086	.020	–	–	–	–
PEF	−.085	.112	–	–	−.060	.002	–	–
PLO	–	–	–	–	−.057	.130	.082	.277
AgL/CUL	–	–	–	–	.055	.099	–	–
NR	–	–	–	–	–	–	−.134	.036
URR	–	–	−.002	.036	–	–	–	–
Constant	−.009		.986		1.303		2.128	
R^2/F	.863	18.004	.884	21.837	.812	21.638	.861	14.719
$\bar{R}^2$	.882		.844		.775		.803	

The fits are very good, $\bar{R}^2$ ranges from 0.78 (Eq. 5.3, APE) to 0.88 (Eq. 5.1, PUP). The most significant poverty raising factors are : Large size of village (ASV), proletarianisation of rural labour (WL), high indebtedness (DAR), social discrimination (SCST) and sex discrimination (SR). Unexpectedly, irrigation (IRR) and non-agricultural development (NONAG) also raise poverty. Poverty reducing factors are: large asset base (CIA), greater use of fertilisers (FERT), larger availability of credit (DAgML, DPMLT), larger budget allocation to food items and large leasing-out by marginal and small farmers (a possible sign of the development of capitalist relations).

Signs of several key variables, specially those related to indebtedness, wage labour and non-agricultural development seem to be perverse. It would be useful to have a close look at them here. The proportion of wage labour, specially in agriculture, is taken to be an indicator of the development of capitalist relations in agriculture. However, in the early phase of development, as was the case in the early seventies, wages would be low, specially in the case of those working as casual workers, hence, poverty is expected to be high. The perverse sign of NONAG might be because this development is very weak or because of the particular definition of the variable. Other variables, specially value added in manufacturing, would be more appropriate, but data at region/district level do not exist. Regarding the perverse signs of indebtedness variables, it should be noted that the data seem to be highly doubtful. A comparison of AIDIS Survey 1971-72 and 1981-82 would confirm it. Many loans are not reported – they simply go underground. (Mehta, 1990 : 71).

Thus, it can be concluded that the best way of alleviating poverty is by strengthening the asset base of the rural households, stepping up the agricultural growth rate and lowering the proportion of casual wage labour and reducing the sex bias in rural areas. The importance of the agricultural moneylenders also highlights the fact that capitalist development can also help in the solution of the problem of absolute poverty by satisfying the credit needs for productive purposes of the rural people. SC and ST people need special attention.

The results obtained with the composite indicator of poverty are similar to the above. $\bar{R}^2$ is again very high (0.844). The variables found to be significant are the same and the t values are also nearly same.

Thus, the results are not sensitive to the choice of the indicator of nutritional inadequacy. However, the relationship of APE with the explanatory variables is not so close. Results obtained with real income indicator is similar in substance to those obtained with the nutritional inadequacy indicators. Hence real income deficiency is a better surrogate indicator of poverty than nominal income or expenditure.

Conclusions

The regression analysis of the determinants of poverty leads us to the identification of the crucial factors influencing poverty in regions of India. The results obtained are mostly on expected lines and are not much sensitive to the particular indicator chosen to represent poverty. However, because of interaction of many of the variables, many surprising results are also obtained, specially regarding the credit market and the development of non-agricultural sector. Many of these might not have arisen if simultaneous equation model of interaction of the variables had been developed.

However, the results also expose the limitations of regression analysis in such studies. It can capture only the unity in diversity. It does not use the richness of data to reveal the highly complex patterns of relationships in which the different structural variables may enter. For this, the case of each individual region has to be discussed separately and in relation to the other regions. This task is attempted in the next chapter.

NOTES

1. For detailed results at state level, see Mehta, (1990).
2. "A country's development prospects are inversely proportional to its natural resource endowment." Ranis (1984 :39-51) See also James, Naya, Meier (1988 : 16).
3. See next chapter for further discussion of leasing activities.
4. D.P. Sharma also finds that marginal farmers are at a disadvantage in comparison to agricultural labourers (1985:55)
5. See also Visaria (1974:13) and Lakdawala (1979). However, Raj Krishna (1980), Sau (1978), Parthasarathy (1978) and Dantwala (1978) find a positive relation between poverty and unemployment.
6. See next chapter for detailed discussion.
7. D.P. Sharma gets similar results (1985:56).
8. These variables are suggested and used by Bardhan (1984 and 1986).
9. Poverty can be hypothesised to depend on income level and other variables which themselves depend on several other variables as well as poverty level. Hence full simultaneous equation modelling may be required. This is beyond the scope of the present study.
10. There are quite large, regional variations in these variables, C.V. being 52.6 and 40.2 respectively. Data about two regions are not available.
11. The results hold for inter-state data in early eighties (Mehta, 1990:68).
12. Sagar and associates (1987) point out the fact that inequality and poverty are neutral with respect to the social class of the landowners.

13. The results are confirmed by inter-state model for early eighties. However, here AWE dominants over other variables (Mehta, 1990:67).
14. The regressions are vastly improved when regions are aggregated into states, signs of all the variables turn out to be as hypothesised. (Mehta, 1990: 69-71) Hence, the need for regional disaggregation. However, even at the state level, the patterns in the early seventies and the early eighties differ substantially.
15. The high C.V. in all the population pressure indicators (DP, gp, PhD), ranging between 433.9 to 764.9 per cent, testify to the very wide regional differences. Regional variations in SR and SURR are much smaller in comparison, yet they are still quite high.
16. For calculation of average spacing, it is assumed that all villages are equally spaced. The formula used is:

    $$ASPACE: \sqrt{A/} \, n\text{-}1$$

    Where, A is the total area of the region and n is the total number of villages in the region.
17. The result also holds in the case of the inter-state model. At the state level, data about instability in agricultural growth are also available. However, the relationship of this variable with poverty is weak (Mehta, 1990:65).

6

REGIONAL VARIATIONS IN AGRARIAN RELATIONS IN INDIA

Introduction

Studies on structure of agrarian relations on regional level have been far and few. Most of the studies have either been too aggregative or too disaggregative (village level). In this chapter, we attempt to develop an understanding of regional agrarian structures on the basis of a multitude of dimensions and try to develop a typology of agrarian relations and structures in India.

I
METHODOLOGY AND DATA

The methodology involves development of appropriate indicators of different aspects of agrarian relations and correlates, relating them in different conditions and using clustering analysis for developing a typology of agrarian relations.

Data thrown up by RBI All India Investment and Debt Survey, NSS and Census are used here. Data relate to 64 regions defined by the NSS.

Agrarian relations are *determined by* the development of forces of production in agriculture and elsewhere as also geo-physical conditions and are reflected in the distribution of land and other assets, tenancy relations, labour and wage market relations and debt and credit relations. We have, therefore, selected the following set of indicators:

Geographical, infrastructure and inputs, agricultural production and productivity, rural labour market (wage) relations, land and resources, tenancy relations, debt and credit relations and finally, social oppression and remoteness.

All the variables are first standardized. Standardized scores of regions are classified into very-very high, very high, high, average, low, very low and very-very low. Clustering technique is applied to derive clusters of regions such that regions within a given cluster are structurally closer to each other than those in different clusters.

II
PARAMETERS OF AGRARIAN RELATIONS

Geophysical Conditions

Geophysical conditions influence agriculture and rural economic and social structure in many ways. Rainfall – its quantity, spread and reliability – affects not only agricultural activities but also the entire way of life. From this point of view, quality of soil is also an important variable. These variables determine the availability of food, and, hence historical population settlement pattern and density. These may ultimately result in increased pressure on land, fragmentation of land, land alienation and pauperisation. However, initial favourable geophysical conditions may also lead to a prosperous diversified economy.

Forces of Production in Agriculture

Agricultural production and productivity and rural income are influenced by geo-physical conditions and development of infrastructure like irrigation, power supply, roads, as well as of science and technology in the form of increased use of modern inputs like fertilisers, improved seeds, pesticides, etc. Some forms of infrastructure development are class-specific. For example, irrigation by tubewells can be resorted to only by the rich farmers. All the above factors directly determine the level of agricultural output per capita as well as per hectare and also the nature of agrarian relations. However, nature of the agrarian relations also influences these factors. Transformation of the agrarian relations depends to a great extent on the development of infrastructure and introduction of new technologies.

Land and Labour Relations

Despite legislation for the abolition of intermediary rights and tenancy reforms, inequality in the distribution of land (owned and operated) is so acute that the problem of poverty can be considered to be the problem of distribution of land. However, skewness in the distribution of land may be observed in various agrarian structures. In the emerging capitalist structure, land alienation takes place and inequalities increase over time, though initially because of land reforms, land might have been distributed more equitably and peasant farming might have resulted. Hence concentration of land has to be looked into in relation to other indicators of agrarian relations. One such indicator is the prevalence of tenancy.

It is generally felt that tenancy is grossly under-reported in order to bypass the various land reform laws.[1] Still the existing data can reveal the basic features. Incidence of high tenancy is generally taken to be an indicator of feudal relation in agriculture. However, various forms of tenancy can exist even under capitalism (Gupta, (1980); Ghosh and Dutt (1977)). In order to understand the nature of exploitation, it is, therefore, necessary to get additional information about the terms of leasing, purpose of leasing, capital or other resources supplied by the landlord, the land position of the landlord and the leasee and the debt on the leasee family and the source and purpose of taking the loan. Heavy loans by the small leasee from the landlord or the agricultural moneylenders primarily for consumption purposes would signify semi-feudal and bondage relation. Bhaduri (1973: 120-137) lists the following as the main features of semi-feudal agriculture: (i) share-cropping, (ii) perpetual indebtedness of the small economic class tenant, (iii) concentration of two methods of exploitation, namely, usuary and land ownership in the hands of the same economic class, lack of accessibility for small tenant to the market. These relations are, therefore, barrier to the introduction of improved technology. If, however, autonomous technology changes take place through the development of infrastructure, the feudal structure will give way to capitalist production relations. If the loans are advanced by the landlord for investment in farm business then this would indicate the beginning of transformation of the semi-feudal relations into capitalist relations. Another form of capitalist penetration is the leasing-in of land by the bigger cultivators. Tenancy may coexist with the increased pace of capitalist farming in these stages of capitalist development. However, ultimately, the landlords or cultivators will take-over cultivation by themselves thus increasing the proportion of agricultural labourers.

A. Ghosh and K. Dutta, (1977: 85-85) trace the path of transition from a purely feudal system of share rent to the modern form of capitalist cultivation, the intermediate forms are characterised by different share tenancies. They identify three modes of production: (i) Semi-feudal (ii) Semi-proletarian peasantry, and (iii) capitalist mode. In contrast, P.C. Joshi (1978: 448-450) identifies some regional agrarian systems and gives a tentative typology: (i) areas of absolute landlordism, (ii) areas of change from non-cultivating landlordism to commercially oriented landlords, or large scale farming by landlords by leasing-out land and providing resources or direct management by the landlords using agricultural labourers evicted by them; (iii) areas of emergence of kulak economy; (iv) areas of predominance of self-employed small and middle peasants and (v) areas of landlessness.

Thus a higher proportion of agricultural labourers to cultivators would signify a higher stage of agricultural development. Doubts have been raised about taking percentage of agricultural labourers in rural population as an indicator of the nature of production relations in agriculture. Many alternative measures have also been suggested. Paresh Chattopadhyaya (1972) recommends free wage labour, Rudra suggests cash wages per acre (A. Rudra: 1970), and R.S. Rao (1970) stresses labour embodied per unit of product as suitable indicators.[2] However, these variables can be handled only at micro-level studies. State and region level data about these variables do not exist. Hence, we stick to the indicator "percentage of male agricultural labourers to male cultivators". A higher proportion of agricultural labourers may be merely hidden tenancy in order to avoid claim on land in future. Moreover, as Bardhan and Rudra (1980: 1477) have shown, many forms of agricultural labour relations can exist. If attached agricultural labourers predominate than it would signify the prevalence of bondage. In this case, the productivity of land will be low.

The Credit Relations

Analysis of agrarian relations lays great emphasis on the relations in the credit market. The source, purpose and the terms of credit indicate the nature and hold of the exploitative classes. Credit is the most potent instrument in the hands of the affluent classes to keep agricultural wages low, to extract large absolute surplus value and to control the marketing of the agricultural produce. Besides this, it acts as a social-political lever. At the same time, modernisation of agriculture requires availability of credit on easy terms.

Initially, professional moneylenders are the main suppliers of credit. Their principal occupation is moneylending. They realise their dues in cash and, in the case of default, take over the movable property (and not land). The objective is to maximise interest income. On the other hand, middle and rich landlords lease-out land to landless and poor tenants extracting high rent. In the absence of default, they also start giving consumption loans. The aim is not to maximise interest income but to maximise the appropriation of output and to ensure nearly free supply of labour. More often than not, the tenants default. This keeps them in perpetual bondage.

However, this type of exploitation has its own limitations. When the state develops infrastructure and new technologies are available and the demand for agricultural products also rises, then the landlords and bigger farmers may use credit as an instrument of increasing output as well as their share of the produce of the debtors. This tends to transform the tenancy relations from pure feudal to semi-capitalist (commercially-oriented landlords) relations where the landlord supplies capital, other inputs and also credit to the tenants and takes larger share of the produce in exchange.

In such a situation, leasing-out land to landless, marginal and small farmers is increasingly found to be less efficient way of accumulation, even usury and bondage put limit on profitability. Then the middle and rich peasantry would try to expand area under cultivation by resuming land for self-cultivation as well as by leasing-in land, on one hand, and by giving loans on usufructuary mortgage. The main objective of this new class of landlords – rich peasantry turned agricultural moneylenders – is not to maximise interest income or rental income but to increase the area of cultivation under it. Hence, a large proportion of loan advanced by them is against security of immovable property under usufructuary mortgage. (All India Rural Debt Survey 1988-89, Vol. 1 part 2, p.3). The first preference of the middle and rich land owners is to evict tenants or buy land by the above process. However, if it is not possible because of existing tenancy and/or ceiling laws, then they will lease-in land, on one hand, and induce their tenants to raise productivity by sharing part of cost, on the other. This tendency of the big landowners-cum-agricultural moneylenders would lead to land alienation of the small and marginal farmers, leading to increasing inequalities in the distribution of land. The end result of all these processes is to pass the effective control of land from the owners of labour to the owners of capital.

Social Oppression and Remoteness

Scheduled Castes and Scheduled Tribes are still socially and economically the most backward and exploited sections of our population. Though class differentials among the Scheduled Castes and Scheduled Tribes have started emerging as more advanced sections and groups among them are able to utilise the various facilities and concessions being granted at all levels of government, the vast masses still remain at the lowest level of existence. Not only this, whenever they have tried to organise for obtaining or retaining the benefits from various programmes of the government they have to face brutal violence from the upper classes and castes. This is specially true in the rural areas.

Though the population of Scheduled Castes and Scheduled Tribes cannot be changed by the policy-makers and, hence, this cannot serve as a policy or target variable, yet inclusion of this indicator in the present analysis is not out of place. The nature and dynamics of the agrarian relations cannot be understood independently of this factor.

All the above facets of rural life in combination determine agrarian and rural socio-economic structure. These variables are interrelated in a very complex manner, each combination leading to a different structure. Various agrarian structures lead to different modes of exploitation, different causes of underdevelopment and poverty and different possible paths of development. The policy-mix in these situations must differ significantly. Hence, there is a need for preparing complete profile of each region, determine its structure and use this knowledge to understand the dynamics of poverty generation.

III
A TYPOLOGY OF AGRARIAN RELATIONS

Different modes may coexist implying different, and often conflicting, trends of development. In this situation the problem of identifying the dominant mode and trends has to be faced. Below, a description of the features of the main modes of production in the present situation in India is given.

1. Feudalism

There is preponderance of small farmers with no ownership or even occupancy right to land. Subsistence leasing on share of crop or fixed rent in kind prevails. No investment on land is made by landlord. Productivity is low. There is highly unequal distribution of ownership holdings as well as very high proportion of owners not operating land, P.C. Joshi (1978: 448-450) terms regions exhibiting these characteristics as areas of absolute landlordism.

2. Semi-feudalism

1. Owners of labour power are independent producers either as owners of land or leasees.
2. Proportion of households operating land is high.
3. Tenancy is high with preponderance of share-cropping.
4. Lesser extent of inequality in respect of size of operational holdings as compared to the size of ownership holdings. Distribution of ownership holdings is less skewed than in feudalism.
5. Proportion of agricultural labourers is low. Unemployment is also low.
6. Proportion of credit supplied by professional moneylenders is high as also that taken for consumption purposes. Average debt may be low since farm investment is low. There is usurious exploitation and perpetual indebtedness of small tenants.
7. Proportion of absentee landlords is relatively high.
8. Land and labour productivity are low. Infrastructure development is low and capital base in weak.

3. Peasant Farming

(Areas of predominance of small and middle self-employed peasants)

1. Owners of labour power are independent producers as owner of land.

2. The proportion of households owning and operating land is very high.
3. Tenancy is low.
4. Proportion of agricultural labourers is low.
5. Inequalities in ownership as well as operational holding are low.

This mode may have some features of semi-feudalism and some of semi-proletarian peasantry. Of course, productivity, farm investment and farm incomes would be low.

4. Semi-Proletarian Peasantry

1. Large landowners become profit-oriented as cities grow and profit can be earned by marketing farm output.
2. Peasant farmers begin to be partly expropriated.
3. There is preponderance of marginal and small farmers.
4. Landlords still do not cultivate land themselves but lease-out land to landless, marginal and small farmers.
5. In order to raise productivity and profit, landlords supply finance or inputs on credit. There is high proportion of credit supplied by landlords. Landlords supply both working and fixed capital.
6. At a latter stage, landlords might be camouflaged as cultivators. Hence, proportion of credit by agricultural moneylenders might also be high.
7. Credit for farm business may be relatively higher than in previous categories.
8. Proportion of absentee landlords is low since landlords have now to reside in the village to transform income from land into capital.
9. The tenants, who are the main debtors in default, may be forced to work on low wages for some time on the landlord's farm. Hence, wages are low.
10. The proportion of agricultural labourers is low.
11. Open unemployment is not high. Productivity is higher than in the preceding categories but is not sufficiently high.

P.C. Joshi (1978) designates such regions as areas of commercially-oriented landlords. In these economies, the two modes of exploitation, namely, usury and landownership are concentrated in the hands of the same landowning class. Hence, Bhaduri (1973: 120-137) terms it as semi-feudal mode.

5. Capitalist Mode

1. In the early stage, the expropriated small and marginal farmers are still attached to the landlord-turned kulaks. However, eventually rural poor become free labour. Proportion of agricultural labourers, specially regular workers, is high. Unemployment may also be high.
2. Because of rapid growth of cities and urban population, demand by industries and industrial labour increases. Agriculture becomes potentially profitable.
3. Leasing-out land by middle and large landowners to landless and poor tenants and extracting surplus from them and keeping them in perpetual bondage is less profitable.
4. Middle and large landowners become cultivators. Proportion of absentee landlords is low.
5. Proportion of land operated by these landowners is very high. This is increased by (i) resuming land for self-cultivation (ii) leasing-in land mainly from small and marginal landowners (iii) giving loans to small and marginal farmers on usufructuary mortgage in the event it is not possible to evict tenants.
6. Hence, the development of infrastructure is high, capital base is relatively strong.
7. Proportion of credit obtained from agricultural moneylenders, specially by marginal and small farmers, is high. However, middle and large landowners obtain credit from institutional agencies.
8. Labour and land productivity is high. Wages are also relatively high.
9. Proportion of landless households may or may not be higher than in the preceding categories, however, the proportion of households not operating land would be very high.
10. Concentration of ownership holdings is expected to be high but concentration of operational holding would be much higher.
11. Leasing may not be low. However, leasing-in would be mainly

by the middle and large landowners and leasing-out by the marginal and small landowners. Though the number of tenants may be small, the area under tenancy would be high.

12. Hence, the proportion of large operators would be high and that of small operators low. Instead of size of ownership holding, size of operational holding becomes the important level of economic, political and social power.
13. Unemployment rate may or may not be high.
14. Share-croppers (marginal and small farmers) and agricultural labourers constitute the main oppressed classes.

Regions exhibiting these characteristics may be subdivided into— (i) the emerging capitalist economies, and (ii) the developed capitalist economies.

In any real situation, none of these modes is expected to exist in pure farm. In a dynamic situation, a variety of intermediate and overlapping categories may exist. However, in every situation, the dominant mode has to be identified in order to understand the correlation of forces and the consequent direction of development in the future.

The necessary conditions for breaking the vicious circle of poverty and stagnation by transformating the feudal agriculture to capitalist agriculture and thereby releasing the forces of production in agriculture may be stated as follows:

(i) Undertaking of basic institutional changes,
(ii) Developing infrastructure,
(iii) Rapid industrialisation, and
(iv) Introduction of new technologies in agriculture to raise productivity.

Cluster Formation : The Typology

Thirty eight structural variables have been considered for forming structurally homogeneous regions. The technique of cluster analysis has been used. The cumulative error sum of squares at steps 10, 20, 30 and 40 is 1.951, 5.23, 10.87 and 23.20 per cent respectively. At step 30, twenty-five clusters are formed of which twelve are single region and thirteen are multi-region clusters. 55 regions (excluding regions 16, 48 and 58 to 64) have been included in the exercise.

The variables used in forming the clusters are:

1. Forces of production in agriculture: OPC. OPH
2. Land relations: AVA, AD, LD, COLA
3. Leasing operations
4. Labour relations
5. Credit relations: CINDI, CINDII, Debt Source (DSC)
6. Population pressure: PD, PhyD, gp
7. Settlement pattern: DU, PSV, ASPACE, ASV
8. Sex-bias: SR
9. Social oppression: SC, ST, SC+ST
   (Full list is given in appendix to chapter 1)

Some more information was also collected after clustering results were obtained. These are: the dependency ratio (DR), agricultural growth rate (AGR) and per cent of working population in non-agricultural sectors (NONAG). This information is also used in describing the nature and structure of the economies of the clusters.

The following structural clusters are formed at step 30. They are rearranged in accordance with cluster formation at step 40.

Cluster No.	Region No.	Cluster No.	Region No.
1	1, 46, 47, 45	11	17
2	3, 35, 2, 24	21	43
3	4, 49	12	18
22	50, 51, 52		
5	6, 21, 22, 37, 38	13	19, 20
4	5	14	23, 24, 41, 42, 44
6	7, 8, 36	15	25
23	53	17	29
7	9	18	31
		19	32
8	10, 33, 12, 27, 13	24	54, 55, 57
16	26	25	56
9	11, 28, 30		
10	14, 15		
20	39, 40		

The clusters and the structural profiles of the regions are given in Table 6.1.

TABLE 6.1: Profile of Agrarian Relations : A Typology

Cluster No.	Region	Region No.	Agricultural Output			Asset & Land Deprivation indicators				Lease Market				
			OPC	OPH	AGR	AVA	AD	LD	COLA	PALL	PLORF	PLO MSF	PLI	PLI SC
			1	2	3	4	5	6	7	8	9	10	11	12
1.	Coastal Andhra Pradesh	(1)	A	VH	L	L	VVH	VH	VVH	VVH	A	L	L	L
	Coastal Southern Tamilnadu	(46)	A	VVH	A	L	VVH	VH	VH	H	A	A	H	A
	Inland Tamilnadu	(47)	A	VH	A	L	VH	VH	VVH	VH	A	A	L	L
	Coastal Northern Tamilnadu	(45)	H	VVH	L	L	VVH	VH	H	VH	L	A	A	A
2.	Inland Southern A.P.	(3)	A	A	L	L	H	A	H	A	A	L	L	A
	Inland Northern Karnataka	(35)	A	L	A	A	A	VL	A	H	H	A	A	A
	Inland Northern A.P.	(2)	L	L	VL	A	H	A	H	A	A	L	VL	L
	Inland Southern Karnataka	(34)	A	H	A	L	H	A	A	A	A	L	A	A

(Contd.)

Note: For definition of variables, See Chapter 1, Appendix 1.
V = Very, H = High, L = Low, A = All region average, — = Data not available

TABLE 6.1 (*Contd.*)

Cluster No.	Region	Region No.	Agricultural Output			Asset & Land Deprivation indicators				Lease Market				
			OPC	OPII	AGR	AVA	AD	LD	COLA	PALL	PLORF	PLO MSF	PLI	PLI SC
			1	2	3	4	5	6	7	8	9	10	11	12
3.	Assam Plains	(4)	L	A	A	L	A	A	VL	L	A	A	VVH	H
	Himalayan Uttar Pradesh	(49)	A	A	A	A	L	VII	A	L	L	L	VH	VH
22.	Western Uttar Pradesh	(50)	H	H	H	H	L	A	L	H	L	A	L	A
	Central Uttar Pradesh	(51)	A	A	A	L	A	A	VL	A	A	A	A	VH
	Eastern Uttar Pradesh	(52)	L	A	A	L	L	H	A	L	L	A	H	H
5.	Southern Bihar	(6)	L	L	L	L	A	A	L	VL	A	VL	VL	L
	Eastern Madhya Pradesh	(21)	A	L	A	L	A	L	A	L	A	A	H	L
	Inland Eastern M.P.	(22)	L	VL	A	L	A	L	L	L	A	A	A	A
	Southern Orissa	(37)	VVL	A	L	VL	VVII	A	A	A	A	A	H	L
	Northern Orissa	(38)	A	A	L	L	II	A	A	L	A	A	H	A
4.	Assam Hills	(5)	A	VII	VII	L	L	L	VL	VL	L	VL	A	L

TABLE 6.1 (*Contd.*)

Cluster No.	Region No.	Credit Market			Social Oppression		Market Labour				Geo-physical & Infrastructure Variables			
		DCI_1	DCI_2	DSC	SC	ST	URR	RFL	AGL/CUL	AWE	NR	CRAIN	SOIL	CII
		13	14	15	16	17	18	19	20	21	22	23	24	25
1.	(1)	H	A	AGML,LL	A	A	H	L	VVH	L	A	VL	H	H
	(46)	H	A	AGML,LL	H	L	VH	VL	VH	A	A	VVL	VVL	VH
	(47)	VH	A	VGML,LL	H	L	A	L	VVH	L	A	VVL	VH	VVH
	(45)	H	A	VGML,LL	VH	L	VH	L	VH	L	A	VVL	VH	VVH
2.	(3)	H	A	AGML,LL	A	L	H	L	A	L	L	L	VH	A
	(35)	H	A	AGML	A	L	H	L	H	L	VL	VH	A	A
	(2)	H	A	VGML.	A	L	H	A	A	L	L	VH	H	A
	(34)	VH	A	AGML,PML, LL	H	L	A	L	L	L	VL	VH	VH	H

(*Contd.*)

Note: DCI_1 = Composite index of indebtedness derived from PDHH, DAR, ADFBT and PIND explaining 74.9 per cent of variance in them Weights: .246, .243, .233 and .274

DCI_2 = Composite index of indebtedness derived from DIA and DFB explaining 88.6 per cent of the variance in them.

CII = Composite index of infrastructure and inputs derived from EP, IRR and FERT, explaining 72.4 of the variance in them. Weights: 305, .329 and .365 (Also see Chapter 5)

TABLE 6.1 (*Contd.*)

Cluster No.	Region No.	Credit Market			Social Oppression		Market Labour				Geo-physical & Infrastructure Variables			
		DCI_1	DCI_2	DSC	SC	ST	URR	RFL	AGL/ CUL	AWE	NR	CRAIN	SOIL	CII
		13	14	15	16	17	18	19	20	21	22	23	24	25
3.	(4)	VL	A	IA	VL	A	L	H	L	VH	H	L	L	L
	(49)	A	L	IA	A	L	VL	A	VL	A	VH	H	VVH	A
	(50)	L	A	AGML,PML	H	L	A	L	A	A	L	A	A	H
	(51)	L	A	AGML	VVH	L	L	A	L	L	A	A	H	A
	(52)	L	A	LL,AGML	H	L	L	A	L	L	A	A	A	A
5.	(6)	VL	L	–	L	VVH	A	A	VL	L	A	A	A	L
	(21)	VL	A	IA	L	VH	L	H	L	VL	H	A	A	L
	(22)	L	A	AGML,PML	L	VH	L	H	L	VL	A	A	VVL	L
	(37)	VL	A	IA	A	VH	L	L	A	L	A	A	A	L
	(38)	VL	A	IA	A	VVH	H	L	L	L	H	A	H	L
4.	(5)	VL	A	PNL	VL	VVH	VL	L	VL	VVH	H	L	L	L

TABLE 6.1 *(Contd.)*

Cluster No.	Region	Region No.	Agricultural Output			Asset & Land Deprivation Indicators				Lease market				
			OPC	OPH	AGR	AVA	AD	LD	COLA	PALL	PLORF	PLO MSF	PLI	PLI SC
			1	2	3	4	5	6	7	8	9	10	11	12
6.	Northern Bihar	(7)	L	A	L	L	A	A	A	A	A	VH	VVH	VVH
	Central Bihar	(8)	L	A	A	A	A	H	A	A	A	VL	VH	VH
	Coastal Orissa	(36)	L	A	A	L	H	VH	A	A	A	H	H	VVH
23.	Southern Uttar Pradesh	(53)	A	L	H	L	A	A	VL	L	A	A	VVH	VVH
7.	Eastern Plains Gujarat	(9)	A	A	H	A	A	L	A	A	A	L	VVL	VL
8.	Plains Northern Gujarat	(10)	H	A	H	H	L	A	A	A	L	L	VL	L
	Inland Eastern Karnataka	(33)	A	VH	A	A	H	A	VVH	A	A	L	L	L
	Dry Area of Gujarat	(12)	H	VL	H	H	L	VL	L	A	A	L	VL	L
	Inland-Western Maharashtra	(27)	VH	VL	VVL	A	A	L	A	L	A	L	VL	L
	South Gujarat	(13)	VVH	A	A	VVH	A	L	A	H	A	L	L	L

(Contd.)

TABLE 6.1 (*Contd.*)

Cluster No.	Region	Region No.	Agricultural Output			Asset & Land Deprivation Indicators				Lease market				
			OPC	OPH	AGR	AVA	AD	LD	COLA	PALL	PLORF	PLO MSF	PLI	PLI SC
			1	2	3	4	5	6	7	8	9	10	11	12
16.	Coastal Maharashtra	(26)	L	H	L	L	H	A	A	L	L	L	A	L
9.	Plains, Southern Gujarat	(11)	A	A	L	A	VH	H	VVH	VVH	A	VL	A	VL
	Inland Northern Maharashtra	(28)	L	VL	VVL	A	H	L	H	A	A	L	L	L
	Inland Eastern Maharashtra	(30)	A	VL	A	A	H	L	H	H	A	A	A	L
10.	Eastern Haryana	(14)	VVH	H	VH	VVH	L	A	A	VVH	A	VVH	A	H
	Western Haryana	(15)	VVH	L	VH	VVH	VL	L	A	H	H	VVH	H	H
	Northern Punjab	(39)	VVH	VH	VVH	VVH	L	H	H	VVH	H	VVH	A	H
	Southern Punjab	(40)	VVH	VH	VVH	VVH	L	L	H	VVH	H	VVH	H	H
11.	Outer Hills of J. & K.	(17)	L	L	VH	H	VVL	A	VL	VL	L	L	L	A
21.	Southern Rajasthan	(43)	L	L	A	A	L	L	VL	VL	L	L	L	L
12.	Jhelum Valley of J. & K.	(18)	A	H	VH	A	VVL	H	VL	VL	L	L	L	A
13.	Northern Kerala	(19)	VL	VH	A	L	H	VVH	A	VL	L	VL	VL	L
	Southern Kerala	(20)	VL	VH	A		A	VVH	H	VL	VH	L	VL	L
14.	Inland Western M.P.	(23)	A	VL	A	A	A	VL	A	A	L	A	L	A
	Western M.P.	(24)	A	L	L	H	L	VL	L	L	L	L	L	L

TABLE 6.1 (*Contd.*)

Cluster No.	Region. No.	Credit Market			Social Opression		Market Labour				Geo-physical & Infrastructure Variables			
		DCI_1	DCI_2	DSC	SC	ST	URR	RFL	AGL/ CUL	AWE	NR	CRAIN	SOIL	CII
		13	14	15	16	17	18	19	20	21	22	23	24	25
6.	(7)	A	A	AGML,LL	A	L	A	L	A	L	A	A	L	A
	(8)	L	L	AGML,LL	H	L	VH	H	A	L	A	A	L	H
	(36)	A	L	LL, AGML	A	L	VVH	L	L	L	H	L	L	A
23.	(53)	H	A	AGML,PML	VH	A	L	A	A	L	L	H	A	L
7.	(9)	A	A	IA	VL	VVH	A	L	A	A	A	H	VVL	A
8.	(10)	VVH	A	–	L	L	A	L	A	A	L	H	VVL	H
	(33)	H	A	–	A	L	A	A	H	A	A	VH	VH	A
	(12)	A	L	IA,AGML	L	L	A	A	A	A	L	H	VVL	A
	(27)	A	A	IA	L	L	A	L	A	A	A	A	A	A
	(13)	H	A	IA	L	L	L	A	A	VH	L	A	L	A
16.	(26)	L	A	–	VL	A	A	A	L	A	VVH	H	H	L

(*Contd.*)

TABLE 6.1 (*Contd.*)

Cluster No.	Region No.	Credit Market			Social Opression		Market Labour				Geo-physical & Infrastructure Variables			
		DCI_1	DCI_2	DSC	SC	ST	URR	RFL	AGL/CUL	AWE	NR	CRAIN	SOIL	CII
		13	14	15	16	17	18	19	20	21	22	23	24	25
9.	(11)	A	A	IA,LL	VL	VVH	L	A	VVH	A	A	H	VL	A
	(28)	A	A	IA	VL	H	VH	A	L	A	VL	A		
	(30)	A	A	IA	VL	L	H	A	VH	A	A	A	H	L
10.	(15)	A	VVL	LL,PMLT	H	L	L	VH	H	A	L	A	H	H
	(15)	A	A	LL,AGML	H	L	L	VH	A	VVH	VL	A	H	A
	(39)	H	A	LL,IA	VVH	L	A	A	VVH	VVH	L	A	VH	VVH
	(40)	H	A	LL,IA	VH	L	L	VH	VVH	VVH	L	A	VH	VVH
11.	(17)	A	H	PML	L	L	VL	VVH	VL	VVH	–	–	–	–
21.	(43)	VVH	A	PMLT	L	VVH	VL	VVH	VL	L	L	A	A	A
12.	(18)	H	A	PMLT	VVL	L	VH	VVH	VL	A	–	–	–	–
13.	(19)	L	A	IA	L	L	VVH	VL	L	H	–	–	–	–
	(20)	H	L	IA	L	L	VVH	VL	VL	H	–	–	–	–
14.	(23)	A	A	PMLT,AGML	A	A	L	A	A	L	A	H	VL	L
	(24)	H	A	PMLT	A	H	A	A	L	L	L	H	VL	L

TABLE 6.1 (*Contd.*)

Cluster No.	Region	Region No.	Agricultural Output: OPC	Agricultural Output: OPH	Agricultural Output: AGR	Asset & Land Deprivation Indicators: AVA	AD	LD	COLA	Lease Market: PALL	PLORF	PLO MSF	PLI	PLI SC
			1	2	3	4	5	6	7	8	9	10	11	12
	Western Rajasthan	(41)	L	VVL	H	H	L	VL	L	L	L	VH	L	L
	Northern Eastern Rajasthan	(42)	A	A	L	VH	H	VL	VL	L	L	A	A	A
	South Eastern Rajasthan	(44)	H	L	H	H	VL	VL	L	L	H	H	H	A
15.	Northern Madhya Pradesh	(25)	L	VL	A	A	L	VL	L	L	L	L	L	L
17.	Inland Central Maharashtra	(29)	H	VVL	VVL	A	A	VL	A	H	A	A	VL	L
18.	Eastern Maharashtra	(31)	A	L	L	A	L	L	A	A	VVH	VVH	L	L
19.	Coastal & Ghats Karnataka	(32)	H	VH	A	L	VH	H	H	H	VVH	VVH	VVH	L
24.	Himalayan West Bengal	(54)	H	H	A	L	VH	H	L	H	A	H	A	A
	Eastern Plains West Bengal	(55)	H	H	H	L	VH	H	A	H	A	H	A	VVH
	Western Plains West Bengal	(57)	A	H	L	L	A	H	A	A	A	A	A	VH
25.	Central Plains West Bengal	(56)	VH	VH	A	L	VH	VVH	H	VH	A	VH	A	VH

TABLE 6.1 *(Contd.)*

Cluster No.	Region No.	Credit Market			Social Oppression		Market Labour				Geo-physical & Infrastructure Variables			
		DCI_1	DCI_2	DSC	SC	ST	URR	RFL	AGL/CUL	AWE	NR	CRAIN	SOIL	CII
		13	14	15	16	17	18	19	20	21	22	23	24	25
	41	VH	A	PMLT,AGML	A	L	L	L	VL	H	VL	H	A	L
	42	H	A	AGML,PMLT	H	A	L	A	L	A	L	L	A	A
	44	VH	A	AGML,PMLT	A	H	VL	VVH	L	L	L	VH	A	A
15.	25	•A	A	PMLT,LL	H	L	L	H	VH	L	L	H	L	L
17.	29	A	A	IA	L	L	A	A	VH	L	L	A	L	L
18.	31	VL	VVL	IA	VL	A	VH	A	L	L	H	H	A	L
19.	32	L	L	IA	VL	L	L	A	VH	A	VVH	VH	VH	L
24.	54	VL	A	LL	VVH	A	A	VH	L	H	VVH	A	L	L
	55	L	A	IA	H	A	H	L	A	A	H	A	L	L
	57	L	A	—	A	A	VH	L	L	A	A	A	A	L
25.	56	L	A	—	VH	L	A	VL	VH	H	H	A	L	A

1.1 *Coastal A.P., Coastal South T.N.; Inland T.N.; and Coastal North T.N.*

Low asset base, vary high asset and land deprivation of the majority of rural population. Very high inequalities in the distribution of land and other assets.

Very high proportion of non-cultivating land-owners, as well as that of agricultural labourers. Average or low leasing activities specially those on share of crop. High indebtedness, proportion of expenditure for meeting out household deficit is average. Agricultural moneylenders and landlords are the main suppliers of credit.

Unemployment is high to very high. Geophysical conditions are extremely favourable and there is relatively very high development of infrastructure. Hence productivity of land is high. However, due to pressure of population on land output per worker is low, wages are also low. High proportion of Scheduled Castes.

Rental exploitation is low: feudal elements are transforming themselves into profit-oriented operators: *Semi-proletarian peasantry mode.*

1.2 *Inland South A.P.; Inland North Karnataka; Inland North A.P.; and Inland South Karnataka*

Low asset base, asset and land deprivation and inequalities are high but lower than in group (1.1).

Proportion of absentee landlords is average, and average leasing activities. Proportion of agricultural labourers is average, however, unemployment is high and wages are low. Geophysical conditions are not favourable and infrastructure development is also average. Hence productivity is low.

High indebtedness but proportion of debt for consumption purposes is at average level. Besides agricultural moneylenders and landlords, professional moneylenders are still the dominant source of credit.

Low rental exploitation though usurious exploitation is high. Movement towards *semi-proletarian peasantry* mode is still very weak.

2.1 *Assam Plains, Himalayan U.P.; Western U.P.; Central U.P.; and Eastern U.P.*

Low asset base. However, in contrast to (1.1) and (1.2) asset and land deprivation and inequalities are low. Proportion of absentee landlords and agricultural labourers are also low, unemployment rate is also low. However, leasing activities, specially, on share of crop are relatively high. Indebtedness is low and there is no unambiguous dominant source of finance. In the first two regions institutional agencies and in rest moneylenders are the dominant source.

Geophysical conditions, infrastructural development, productivity and wages are average. Rental exploitation still exists. *Peasant (small* and middle) *farming economies.*

2.2 *South Bihar; East M.P.; Inland Eastern M.P.; South Orissa; and North Orissa*

Low asset base, low land deprivation and inequality except in Orissa in which asset deprivation is very high. Proportion of absentee landlords is low. Leasing activities are high except in South Bihar but not on share of crop.

Proportion of agricultural labourers is low as is unemployment rate and indebtedness, forces of production are not well developed. Hence, productivity and wages are low.

These are essentially *tribal economies* – lowly developed stagnant economies, essentially *pre capitalist* in nature and credit starved.

3. Assam Hills

This region is not linked to any other region. Though average value of assets is low, inequalities in the distribution of land and assets are also very low. Absentee landlordism and leasing activities are at low level. Proportion of agricultural labourers is very low, unemployment rate is also very low. Indebtedness is also low. The dominant source of credit is professional moneylenders.

However, productivity and wages are relatively high, this is in the context of low infrastructure development but favourable rain conditions. The regional economy can be characterised as a *tribal peasant farming* economy though at a relatively high level of development and productivity.

4.1 *North Bihar; Central Bihar; and Coastal Orissa*

Asset base is weak. Inequalities in the distribution of land assets are average or high. Proportion of non-cultivating land owners is average. The most distinguishing characteristic of the region is very high leasing activities, mostly on share of crop – an indicator of the prevalence of *feudal land relations*.

The proportion of agricultural labourers is average or low. Unemployment rate is very high. Though geophysical condition, infrastructure development and land productivity are average, productivity per worker is low.

Agricultural moneylenders and landlords are the major sources of credit.

These regions show signs of *semi-feudal agrarian* relations. The situation is worsened by high population pressure.

4.2 *Southern U.P.*

This region is also similar to the above three regions in most of the characteristics. However, unemployment rate is low and proportion of scheduled castes is very high. This, again, characterises a *semi-feudal economy*.

5. Gujarat-Eastern Plains

In this region, most of the structural variables are at the all India average level. However, leasing activities are at very low level. This is predominantly *tribal economy* which has shaken-off feudal relations.

6.1 *North Gujarat Plains; Inland Eastern Karnataka; Gujarat Dry Areas; Inland Western Maharashtra; and South Gujarat*

Asset base is relatively strong, best being in South Gujarat, average or low concentration of land and other assets except in Inland Eastern Maharashtra, where it is very high. Proportion of agricultural labourers is also average, however, leasing activities are quite low. Credit is adequately provided by the institutional agencies. Productivity is high and wages average.

These seem to be *peasant farming economies*.

6. Coastal Maharashtra

Nearly all variables are at all India average or lower levels. It is a *peasant farming economy.*

6.3 *South Gujarat Plains; Inland North Maharashtra; and Inland Eastern Maharashtra*

Asset base is average, however asset deprivation is high and inequalities in the distribution of land and assets are quite high. Alongwith this, absentee landlordism is also high but leasing activities are at a low level. Naturally, proportion of agricultural labourers in farm working population is very high. Geophysical conditions and infrastructural development are at the all India average, so also labour productivity and wages. A case of *nascant agrarian capitalism.*

7.1 *Eastern Haryana; Western Haryana; and Himachal Pradesh*

Asset base is very high, asset and land deprivation is low, inequalities in the distribution of assets and income are average. Absentee landlordism is high, leasing is high, mainly marginal and small farmers lease-out land but they do not lease-in land. There is average credit availability financed by landlords and moneylenders. The proportion of agricultural labourers is high and productivity and wages are very high. the economy is *advancing towards agrarian capitalism.*

7.2 *North Punjab; and South Punjab*

It reflects the most advanced stage of development of agrarian capitalism. Average value of assets with households is very high, asset and land deprivation is low; however, inequalities are high (in contrast to Haryana). Absentee landlordism is very-very high but leasing-out by marginal and small farmers is also very high and proportion of agricultural labourers is also very high, credit availability is high, and institutional agencies are dominant suppliers of credit. Productivity and wages are very high.

Delhi (61) lies somewhere between cluster (7.1) and (7.2). *Advanced agrarian capitalism.*

8.1 *Outer Hills of Jammu and Kashmir*

Average value of assets is high, deprivation is low and, inequalities are very low, leasing activities are also low; absentee landlordism is very low, proportion of agricultural labourers is also very low, adequate credit is available financed by professional moneylenders, but productivity and wages are low and unemployment is also low.

It is *low productivity peasant economy.*

8.2 *South Rajasthan*

Though geographically quite away and different from Outer Hills of J&K, its agrarian structure is, in most parts, similar to that region.

Asset base is average, land and asset deprivation is low and inequalities very low, leasing activities and use of wage labour in agriculture are very low; productivity and wages are also low. Unemployment is low. Indebtedness is very high financed by professional moneylenders and traders.

It is predominantly a *peasant farming tribal economy* subject to *severe usurious exploitation.*

8.3 *Jhelum Valley of Jammu and Kashmir and Mountaneous Jammu and Kashmir*

Asset base is average with low to very low inequalities in the distribution of land and other assets. Leasing activities are also very low. Use of agricultural labourers is very low. Productivity and wages are average. Indebtedness is high, credit is supplied predominantly by professional moneylenders and traders. The major difference with 8.1 and 8.2 is that unemployment rate is very high in this cluster.

This is *peasant farming economy with usurious exploitation.*

9. North Kerala and South Kerala

Asset base is low and inequalities in the distribution of land and assets are very high. Unemployment is also very-very high. All types of leasing activities are very low and proportion of agricultural labourers is also low. Though productivity per hectare is quite high yet, because of pressure of population on land, productivity per worker is low. Because of organisation of workers, wages are relatively high. Credit is financed mainly by institutional agencies.

Feudal agrarian relations seem to have been completely transformed. Though *capitalism is weak*, its prospects are bright.

10. *Western M.P.; Inland Western M.P.; Western Rajasthan; North Eastern Rajasthan; and South Eastern Rajasthan*

Asset base is average, inequalities are average or low, absentee landlordism is also low. Leasing activities are low in the first three regions and high in South Eastern Rajasthan where leasing-out by marginal and small farmers is dominant. Unemployment is low and use of agricultural labourers is also low. Productivity and wage rates are low. Professional and agricultural moneylenders and traders are the main suppliers of credit which is on high side.

These characterise *peasant farming economies* where usurious exploitation is also prevalent. However, North Eastern and South Eastern Rajasthan are *moving towards capitalism* in Agriculture. All these regions were previously citadels of feudalism.

11. *Northern Madhya Pradesh*

Average asset base with low land and asset deprivation and very low inequalities in distribution of land and assets. Very low unemployment, low leasing activities. However, use of agricultural labourers is very high. Productivity is low. Average credit needs satisfied by professional moneylenders, traders and landlords.

This is evidence of *semi-feudal economy transforming itself into agrarian capitalism*. Usurious exploitation is prevalent.

12.1 *Eastern Maharashtra*

Average asset base, low or average resource deprivation and inequalities. However, unemployment and use of agricultural labourers are very high. Leasing activities are low. Very low loan utstanding which is taken predominantly from institutional agencies. Low productivity, low wages.

Peasant farming economy in transition to capitalist agriculture.

12.2 *Inland Central Maharashtra*

Average asset ase with average asset deprivation and inequalities, land deprivation is low. Unemployment is low (Contrast with 12.1), leasing activities are low, however, proportion of agricultural labourers is very high. Average loan outstanding taken mostly from institutional agencies. High per worker output but low land productivity and wages.

Except for higher unemployment and larger debt, this region is similar to (12.1).

12.3 *Coastal and Ghats of Karnataka*

Low asset base with very high land and asset deprivation and inequalities (contrast with 12.1 and 12.2). Low unemployment. Very-very heavy leasing activities, specially leasing-out by marginal and small farmers is very-very high but not on share of crop. Percentage of agricultural labourers is also very high. Productivity is high, indebtedness is low. Institutional agencies are the dominant source of credit.

All these characterise *capitalist agriculture* that too *quite developed* one.

13.1 *Himalayan West Bengal; Eastern Plains W.B.; and Western Plains W.B.*

Low asset base but high to very high deprivation and low to average inequalities. Average leasing activities but mostly on share of crop. Proportion of agricultural labourers is low but unemployment rate is high. Geophysical conditions are average but infrastructure development is low. Still productivity is high and earnings of agricultural labourers are high. Indebtedness is low, financed by institutional agencies. Proportion of Scheduled Caste is high. It is difficult to characterize these economies; feudal exploitation is still prevalent and capitalism is emerging: may be characterised as *Semi-proletarian peasantry* mode.

13.2 *Central Plains West Bengal*

Low asset base but very high assets and land deprivation and inequalities in the distribution of land and assets. However, average unemployment, average infrastructure development, absentee landlordism is very high, leasing out by marginal and small farmers is very high though overall leasing activities are average, but heavily on share of crop.

Proportion of agricultural labourers is very high, mostly casual. Productivity is very high and thus wages and earnings in agriculture are also very high. There are diverse sources of credit.

All these identify quite *advanced capitalist agriculture*.

14. *Manipur Plains, Manipur Hills, Tripura, and Meghalaya*

Low asset base. Average resource deprivation except in Tripura, low proportion of agricultural labourers. Low to very low leasing activities. Credit is mostly provided by institutional agencies. Debt condition is average. Essentially *tribal peasant farming economies*.

Conclusion

Thus, different regions show different patterns of agrarian relations. Even regions within a State exhibit different relations. Hence, the dynamics of different regions would vary so also the problems and solutions thereof.

NOTES

1. See Frankel (1978:98), Mehta and Prashad (1988:41), A. Gupta (1980: A-98-102) and Athreya et al (1987).
2. This analysis involves the discussion of the concept of agrarian class. Athreya (1987: 147-190) examines the alternative methods of identifying the class status of individual households. He prefers surplus and its appropriation criterion to the exploitation, ownership or tenancy criteria as suggested by Utsa Patnaik and others.

7

SUMMARY, CONCLUSIONS AND POLICY IMPLICATIONS

I
SUMMARY OF RESULT AND CONCLUSIONS

Introduction

Poverty in rural India remains the most formidable challenge to development. The questions relating to evolving the right mix of policies and appropriate strategies to alleviate poverty in rural areas are being addressed at different levels.

Though different programmes launched by the Central and State Governments have helped in easing the problem to some extent, atleast in the short run, there is still no firm, effective and universally accepted policy prescription.

Approaches to the problem of poverty can be classified into three broad categories : (i) structural, (ii) developmental, and (iii) egalitarian. Structural approach focusses on the processes generating poverty and not on defining and measuring it and then identifying the poor which is the focal point of the egalitarian approach. The developmental approach to poverty relies on the 'trickle down' hypothesis. While it is difficult to agree with the developmental and egalitarian approaches, specially if the objective is to solve the problem of poverty on permanent basis, since the present policies of the Government of India are based on these approaches, the problem of defining and measuring poverty is also handled in this study.

Measurement of Poverty and Method of Analysis

It is, however, almost impossible to capture all dimensions of poverty by a single scaler index, be it per capita income or percentage under poverty line defined on the basis of a calorie norm, or quality of life. Hence, poverty profiles of regions and states have been prepared on the basis of several indicators depicting absolute and relative poverty. Four sets of measures of poverty are used in this study:

1. Nutritional Inadequacy
2. Income Insufficiency
3. Resource Deprivation
4. Low Quality of Life

Average dietary energy requirement (DER) of 1920 calories per capita per day has been used to define ultra-poverty line and percentage of the ultra-poor has been calculated using the head-count ratio for regions in India pertaining to period 1972-73. Alternative methods for preparing indicators of poverty have also been used. In all, 17 indicators are used to represent the different aspects of poverty.

After examining the likely relationship between a list of geophysical, demographic and structural correlates and poverty on *a priori* basis, an empirical regression analysis has been attempted to establish relationship between these variables and poverty, specially nutritional inadequacy, nominal income, real income and composite indicator of poverty at the regional level.

Cluster formation technique is used to prepare a typology of poverty. Poverty profiles of all the regions have been prepared on the basis of standardised scores on different variables.

Results about Relation Between Poverty Measures

It has been found that the distribution of regions in accordance with poverty line defined for different poverty norms is not sensitive either to poverty norm or to the method of calculation. Most of the nutrition based poverty indicators are highly intercorrelated. However, percentage expenditure on food is not correlated with poverty indicators. There are large inter-regional variations in the poverty pattern as reflected by very high coefficient of variation. In India as whole, on an average, 34.8 per cent of rural households were under the ultra-poverty line. The same for the calorie norm of 2400 is 62.8 per cent. It has also been found that there was very high disparity in the distribution of income among the rural population of the regions. The same is true of the distribution of income among the poor.

Resource deprivation measured in terms of the percentage of households having assets less than Rs. 2500 and land less than 2.5 acres is also very high. Fifty-eight per cent of the rural households are land-poor and 32 per cent asset-poor. There are vast inter-regional differentials in this respect too. Another aspect of asset distribution is the concentration of implements in the hands of the rich households. The coefficient of variation here is as high as 74.7 per cent.

Quality of life is measured by survival ratio, female literacy rate and percentage of Kutcha houses. All these happen to be mutually uncorrelated. Thus, no firm conclusion can be derived regarding quality of life. It has been found that poverty (per cent ultra-poor population) is correlated with survival ratio and female literacy. However, the sign of the relationship with literacy ratio is against the usual hypothesis that literacy is negatively correlated with poverty.

State level data indicate that there has been a sharp decline in rural poverty ratio in 1983-84 as compared to 1977-78. However, the results may be highly deceptive, since 1983-84 was an exceptionally good rain/agricultural year nearly all over the country. In spite of this sharp fall in the poverty ratio, the inter-state poverty pattern remains essentially unchanged over the period except in Kerala and one or two other states.

Thus, the regional pattern of poverty is sensitive to the poverty aspect (resources, income, nutrition or quality of life) chosen but is not sensitive to the nutrition norm chosen or the formula used for calculating the poverty index.

Geophysical Conditions, Agrarian and Demographic Structure and Poverty : Regression Results

Since, the trickle-down theory has not been found to be true in all areas in rural India, focus has shifted to pressure on land, highly skewed distribution of land and other productive assets, low productivity in agriculture, absence of dynamism in agriculture, lack of diversification of the economy and exploitative land and credit relations. A major influence on poverty levels is the nature of agrarian structure. Despite several land reforms, the structure remains highly inegalitarian and exploitative. Hence, in many parts of the country even the modest gains in productivity have been insufficient to raise the demand for and earnings of labour.

Factors that influence the level of poverty in different states and regions can broadly be classified into four groups:

1. The level of development of socio-economic infrastructure so as to overcome the geophysical constraints on development.
2. Historically given social, cultural and demographic situation.
3. Ownership of income generating assets (land, labour, human resources) : average level and distribution over households and groups. These are controlled by the working of the land, labour and credit markets.
4. Access to a minimum bundle of goods and services without requiring any change in the ownership of assets — welfare programmes, dual pricing policies, creation of institutional agencies etc. (ILO 1986: 7).

To establish cause and effect relationship between demographic, geophysical and structural variables and poverty, regressions were run taking each block of variables separately. From this analysis it has been found that poverty in the regions is influenced by a few variables only.

Poverty, specially nutritional inadequacy, is expected to be high in regions with high deficit rainfall, high asset and land deprivation, high unemployment, high proportion of wage labour and casual workers in total working population, high debt asset ratio, population pressure, sex ratio (gender-bias) and proportion of SC and ST in the population. Similarly, it is low in regions with high composite indicator of assets, development of infrastructure, output per worker and agricultural growth rate. However, some exceptional results are also obtained. Poverty is also high in regions with high agricultural output per hectare. The trickle-down hypothesis is not supported and, simultaneously, population pressure affects poverty situation adversely.

Leasing activities are not of much importance in determining poverty level. Leasing-out by marginal and small rural households reduces poverty. Regions reporting large loans outstanding, taken even from agricultural moneylenders and professional moneylenders, show lower poverty. It implies that in many regions private moneylenders are making credit available for productive purposes. In contrast, credit starvation seems to be a cause of poverty. Provision of credit by institutional agencies is not sufficient for poverty reduction.

Another unexpected result is that regions exhibiting diversification of the economy in terms of non-agricultural employment also show higher poverty. Thus, the present magnitude and nature of industrial and non-agricultural development does not have significant effect on rural poverty.

The above results emerge when we regress poverty on each block of indicators separately. If we include all these significant explanatory variables together and re-run regression, then a very small number of variables can be identified. Strong asset base, high fertiliser use and credit availability from agricultural moneylenders reduce ultrapoverty as measured by the head-count ratio significantly. High proportion of SC and ST, high wage labour and large size of villages raise ultrapoverty significantly. If we take the composite indicator of poverty in place of the head-count ratio (PUP) then sex ratio (SR) and non-agricultural development also become significant poverty raisers. Rural unemployment rate also gains important explaining power. The overall explaining power. R^2 in the case of ultra-poverty, composite indicator of nutritional poverty and real income is as high as 0.88, 0.84 and 0.80, respectively.

Poverty Clusters

Clustering of regions in accordance with the seventeen indicators of poverty leads to thirteen poverty clusters.

(1) *Cluster No. 1* consists of Northern Kerala and Southern Kerala showing very-very high poverty in all respects, specially nutritional poverty and unemployment.

Coastal Maharashtra, Coastal and Ghats of Karnataka, Northern Orissa, Coastal Northern Tamil Nadu, Western Plains of West Bengal, Central Plains of West Bengal and Southern Orissa may also be placed in this cluster.

(2) *Cluster No. 2* is also a high poverty cluster consisting of Southern Bihar, Eastern Gujarat, Northern Karnataka, Southern Rajasthan and Eastern Maharashtra.

(3) *Cluster No. 3* is also of high poverty consisting of North

Western Maharashtra, Inland Northern Maharashtra and Inland Eastern Maharashtra.

(4) Coastal Andhra Pradesh, Coastal Southern and Inland Tamil Nadu, Southern Gujarat Plains, Inland Eastern Karnataka, Coastal Orissa and Himalayan West Bengal form a cluster of average to high poverty. Eastern Plains of West Bengal, with high poverty, can be added to this cluster.

(5) South Eastern Rajasthan, Eastern Uttar Pradesh and Western Uttar Pradesh form one cluster of low poverty.

(6) Tripura, Central Uttar Pradesh. Manipur Plains, Manipur Hills and Meghalaya form another cluster of low poverty.

(7) Western and Eastern Haryana, Himachal Pradesh, Northern Punjab, Southern Punjab, Delhi and outer Hills of Jammu and Kashmir form a homogeneous cluster of very-very low poverty.

(8) Northern Madhya Pradesh, North Eastern Rajasthan, Jhelum Valley of Jammu and Kashmir and Goa, Daman and Diu also form a cluster of very low poverty.

Western Rajasthan is a class in itself. Nutritional inadequacy is very low. However, this is achieved by a high per cent expenditure on food (PEF). As a result, quality of life is very low.

The remaining sixteen regions are grouped into five clusters of average poverty.

On the basis of Lipton's two 80 per cent criterion, Eastern Plains of Gujarat, Coastal and Ghats of Karnataka, Southern Orissa, Southern Bihar, Southern Rajasthan and Western Plains of West Bengal may be treated as having acute poverty problem. These regions have high proportion of families that are not able to meet even 80 per cent of the calorie requirements even after allocating more than 80 per cent of the budget to food. Inland Northern A.P., Northern Bihar, Central Bihar, Northern Plains of Gujarat, Eastern Maharashtra, Inland Northern Karnataka and Himalayan U.P. have average poverty achieved by high budget allocation to food, hence they can also be considered to be highly vulnerable regions. In contrast, Inland Eastern M.P., Western Rajasthan and Manipur have low poverty but high PEF. This may be a transitional feature or may be because of a particularly bad monsoon year. Kerala and South Plains of Gujarat have very high poverty but very low PEF. Other regions following the above pattern are : Inland Western, Northern and Eastern Maharashtra and Coastal Maharashtra, Tripura and Coastal Northern Tamil Nadu. The poverty situation in these regions can be considered to be less precarious than in the regions mentioned earlier.

Eastern Haryana, Himachal Pradesh, Meghalaya and Delhi are the best regions on the basis of the two-80 per cent criterion.

In terms of all the poverty indicators taken together, Coastal Tamil Nadu, Coastal A.P., Coastal Orissa, Northern Orissa, Himalayan West Bengal, Western Plains of W.B. and Eastern Plains of W.B. are the main sufferers. Others in the group but with low PEF are Kerala, Coastal Northern Tamil Nadu, Northern Maharashtra and Inland Eastern Maharashtra. Poverty eradication in these regions is a really difficult task. These regions should receive the greatest attention of the planners.

Structure of Agrarian Relations and Poverty

For the formulation of an effective policy-mix, it is necessary to identify the structural causes of poverty in these regions. The picture of poverty and its correlates is quite complex. However, some types can be identified on the basis of the poverty and structural profiles of the regions presented in Chapter IV and VI.

Kerala, Coastal Ghats of Karnataka, Southern and Eastern Rajasthan, and Central Plains of West Bengal have high land productivity but low productivity per worker. Hence population pressure is very acute in these regions. Clearly the main problem in these regions is not of raising productivity. The policy package should include development of non-agricultural sectors and strengthening of worker-power to enable them get more employment with higher wages.

Both regions of *Kerala* have high development of the forces of production in agriculture as well as other sectors. Capitalist agriculture is developing but, because of acute population pressure, inequalities in the distribution of assets and income, high unemployment rate and exploitation of labour, the poverty situation is serious. Organised political and trade union action for reducing inequalities and wage exploitation is called for. Migration of the skilled and semi-skilled population can also ease the situation. The undisputedly very high quality of life in the state provides opportunities for these alternatives. Exactly this seems to have happened during the period after 1971 so that poverty has been reduced substantially in the state.

Inland Northern A.P., Southern Bihar, Inland Northern Maharashtra, Eastern Maharashtra, and Coastal and Southern Orissa have low land as well as worker productivity. Growth rate of agricultural output is also low. Hence the urgent necessity in these regions is to identify the causes of this phenomenon and direct policy towards raising productivity.

Coastal A.P., Eastern Plains of Gujarat, Coastal Southern and Northern Tamil Nadu, Inland Western Maharashtra, Kerala, Goa, Daman and Diu, Eastern Plains, Central Plains and Western Plains of W.B. and Northern Orissa have very high proportion of casual wage workers and also high poverty. Thus they suffer from exploitation of workers.

Coastal A.P., Inland, Coastal South and Coastal North Tamil Nadu are in many respects similar to Kerala. However, in these regions usurious exploitation is also very acute. In contrast, in Southern and Northern Orissa, the main problems are those of low level of development of infrastructure and high rental as well as casual labour exploitation. There is also credit starvation as well as high exploitation of the tribal people. Some kind of bondage cannot be ruled out. Almost all household budget is spent on food. The economies are caught in the low equilibrium trap.

Feudal exploitation represented by high proportion of non-cultivating landowners is dominant cause of high poverty in *Coastal Andhra Pradesh, Coastal Northern and Southern Tamil Nadu, Inland Tamil Nadu, Plain Southern Gujarat, Himalayan West Bengal, Central Plains and Eastern Plains of West Bengal* High leasing-out by rich land owners is the main cause of poverty in *South Kerala, Eastern Maharashtra and Coastal and Ghats of Karnataka* and high leasing-in on share of crop is dominant cause in the rest of *West Bengal*. In all these regions, the thrust of the policy ought to be on effective land reforms. In fact, state level analysis would suggest that atleast in *West Bengal and Kerala* this has been done in the period between 1971 and 1983.

All regions of *West Bengal* suffer from multiple adverse factors : low level of development of infrastructure, high resource deprivation, high population pressure, high unemployment and large rental exploitation as well as labour exploitation. The landlords are, however, turning towards productive activities. *Central Plains* region is exceptional in the sense that it has very high level of non-agricultural development still it has high poverty. Other regions do not have high degree of diversification of the economy. Development of infrastructure has to be given top priority. However, more important is political action in reducing inequalities in the distribution of resources.

In *Maharashtra* (except Coastal and Eastern regions), the main problem is that of developing infrastructure specially biased in favour of the poor and reducing wage exploitation of the large number of the casual workers.

Asset formation has to be given top priority in the asset poor high poverty regions. In this respect all regions of *West Bengal* other than *Eastern Plains, Coastal A.P., Coastal and Coastal Northern Tamil Nadu, Northern Orissa, Coastal and Ghats of Karnataka, Coastal Maharashtra and Southern Bihar* are the problem areas. In most of these regions population pressure in terms of the density of population is also serious. Of the specially poverty stricken regions, *Eastern Plains of Gujarat and Coastal Northern Tamil Nadu* have also experienced rapid population growth during the past decade.

Of the nine very high poverty regions, eight have high sex ratio — *Kerala, Coastal A.P., Inland Western Maharashtra, Eastern Maharashtra, Coastal South Tamil Nadu, South Bihar and Goa* have high gender-bias in poverty. Special efforts will have to be directed towards improvement in the condition of the women in these regions.

High poverty due to the very high proportion of the tribal people is a significant factor in *Eastern Plains of Gujarat, Eastern and Southern Rajasthan, Southern Plains of Gujarat, North Orissa and Inland Northern Maharashtra.* Socially oppressed scheduled castes are important factor in the poverty situation in *Coastal and Coastal South Tamil Nadu and Himalayan, Eastern Plains and Central Plains of West Bengal.* In other regions of concentration of these sections, the main cause of poverty is not social oppression, other sections of population are equally likely to be poor.

In *Eastern Gujarat, Eastern Maharashtra and Southern Rajasthan*, there is very heavy concentration of tribals. These are traditional tribal small farming economies working at low level of productivity. There is severe usurious exploitation and also credit starvation for productive purposes. At present, inequalities do not pose much problem. Social reforms are urgently needed to prevent the tribals from falling into the debt trap. Infrastructure development and diversification of the economies should receive top priority. *Eastern M.P., Inland Eastern M.P. and Southern Bihar* have poverty profiles similar to the above regions but the situation is slightly less grave. These are essentially pre-capitalist tribal economies.

Inland A.P., Inland Southern A.P., Inland Southern Karnataka, Northern Karnataka and possibly Goa have transitional semi-proletarian peasant economies lacking in dynamism. The main problem is that of reducing usurious exploitation as well as the exploitation of the casual workers. High vulnerability to monsoon failure complicates the poverty situation.

Though *North Bihar, Central Bihar and Coastal Orissa* have only all India average nutritional poverty level, this is achieved with very high budget allocation to food by the rural households. In these essentially semi-feudal rural economies, there is very high rental as well as wage exploitation. Population pressure is also very high. Thus these economies are also in a highly vulnerable situation.

Punjab, Haryana, Himachal Pradesh, Delhi and Western U.P. are characterised by advanced and dynamic agrarian capitalism. They exhibit low poverty on the basis of nearly all indicators. *Western M.P., Inland Western M.P., North-Eastern and South Eastern Rajasthan* are small and middle peasant farming economies and are moving towards agrarian capitalism. Poverty is at average or low level.

Other regions are difficult to put into types.

It should, however, be noted that despite these differences, the distribution of assets is highly skewed against the poor in almost all regions and the 30 to 40 per cent of households in the lowest strata have practically no productive assets. Again, in most regions, atleast 40 per cent of the rural population is under the poverty line. The necessity of asset formation by these households is thus obvious.

Another fact to be noted with interest is that the poverty and structural clusters do not fall neatly into the various agro-climatic types derived by several geographers, specially by Singh and Singh (1986: 75-88) and Roy (1986: 148-155). Hence, there are no particular reasons to repeat the poverty exercises for zonal groupings as was done by Rao and associates (Rao, 1986: 101-106).

II
POLICY IMPLICATIONS OF THE RESULTS

The above results establish two basic facts:

(i) There cannot be any single index of poverty.

(ii) Whichever, poverty indicators are used, they cannot help in fully understanding the processes of poverty generation in the absence of an understanding of the rural economic structures and agrarian relations. Policy implications can be brought out only by obtaining a grasp of the dynamics of the rural economic structures.

As is clear from this study, the regional pattern of rural agrarian relations and poverty is highly heterogeneous. Hence, the policies for poverty alleviation should also be regionally differentiated. However, identifying the poor and giving them economic support can hardly be an effective solution. This is amply borne out by the past experience.

Despite land reforms and special campaigns like 20-point programme, the "agrarian structure remains highly unequal. Inequalities in rural incomes and land distribution have accentuated poverty. . . . In all, the basic determinants of rural poverty remain unchanged, and while levels of poverty may fluctuate and show occasional improvement, the conditions of rural poor remains highly vulnerable" (I.L.O. 1986:4). Moreover, in regions where disparities within the land system have greatly moderated and led to peasant economies, the situation has not improved much. The bulk of poor are not in a position to derive benefits from extension, credit, research and marketing and processing services (Tarlok Singh, 1988: 6-7). As a result, in these regions small and marginal farmers as well as tenant cultivators form the bulk of the poor. Policy prescriptions in the above two situations will, naturally, vary. In the latter case emphasis has to be on productivity raising and credit and service oriented activities, whereas in the former case land distribution reforms have to carried out.

In most regions, the unemployment rate is far below the poverty ratio. Thus, the unemployment data are of doubtful reliability. They are supposed to measure both open unemployment and underemployment on the basis of persons working or available for work. A rate of unemployment of only 5.08 per cent in terms of person years in the case of Western Rajasthan is clearly an under-estimate as can be judged from the fact that in most parts of the region only single crop is taken. People may not report availability for work simply because they do not expect to get work. In summers, in Western Rajasthan, most people, along with their animals, migrate in search of water and pastures. Obviously, they might have been treated as employed, however, this is obviously distress migration for survival. Similarly, an unemployment figure of 1.10 per cent in the case of Southern Rajasthan region which is tribal is also misleading. However, the discrepancy between the poverty ratio and the rate of unemployment implies that the wage earners are getting below subsistence wages and, the self-employed, though working for most of the time, are not able to produce enough to rise above the poverty line, and even if they are producing enough for survival, a large part is taken away by the landlords or the creditors.

The crux of the problem is, therefore, to identify region specific sets of policies and programmes which would raise agricultural wages, increase the size of land owned and operated by the poorest households, strengthen the asset base of these households, raise their productivity, reduce the appropriation of their output by others, provide supplementary income to the self-employed and create additional jobs outside agriculture. Of course, the policy-mix will vary for different states and regions.

The structural-institutional approach was adopted during the initial period of planning in India and was supplemented by the developmental approach. This did succeed in raising the rate of growth of the economy and agricultural output in particular. However, the differential patterns of implementation of the various land reform legislations and regional differentials in the developmental efforts led to diverse patterns of agrarian relations. Alongwith it, the number of unemployment persons rose alarmingly. Bad monsoons, after-effect of wars with China and Pakistan, high inflation rates and the emerging powerful groups in the rural side led to the complete abandoning of the structural-institutional approach. There was a change in the developmental approach too. The focus of attention was changed from general agrarian development to development of specific crops, specific areas and specific groups of persons called progressive farmers. The stress was on the individual initiative of the farmers supported, of course, by the Government and credit agencies. This class and scale specific strategy did push up the rate of growth in the chosen areas and crops, however, it was at the cost of other areas and crops. Thus, the overall rate of growth of agricultural output stagnated and regional and inter-personal inequalities increased. This increased the economic and political power of the middle and rich 'progressive peasantry' immensely simultaneously raising the consciousness of the rural poor about the gulf between the possibilities and reality. The rising economic and political power of the middle and rich peasantry has been well documented by political scientists as well as economists. However, the growing restiveness of the poor has not been studied as yet except for the rise of the naxalite movement. The various land grab movements, the growing violence on the Scheduled Castes and Scheduled Tribes, the shifting polling pattern of these sections and the increased number of class based actions by them do indicate this restiveness. Because of these factors and the adverse effect of the stagnant agrarian economy in many parts of the country on the overall performance of the economy, the policy-makers have been forced to give attention to specific egalitarian programmes directed towards the poverty stricken groups and regions, while still continuing with the old strategy of development (Rudra, 1979: 72-108).

While these programmes have achieved some success in some areas, their utility as effective programmes of poverty eradication is limited since for covering the targetted population very large transfers of financial and physical resources would have to be mobilised. In the existing property relations in rural India, specially in states like Bihar, Orissa and many parts of the other states, such transfers are politically impossible to undertake. There are bound to be leakages, diversions, intrusions by the richer sections, sabotage and outright opposition (Guhan 1980, Mehta 1980: 17-19). It has been shown that even to the extent these programmes have been implemented, they have failed to pull-up the poor households over the poverty line. No doubt, these may improve the economic condition of some sections of the poor for a while. However, given the existing property relations and the bias of the development strategy which flows from these relations, these very sections are most likely to relapse back into the same rut.

Action based on the above three approaches resulted in different patterns of development and underdevelopment in different regions. Hence, we find regions like *Coastal Maharashtra, Coastal and Ghats of Karnataka and Central Plains of West Bengal* which are relatively highly industrialised and yet are lagging in agricultural growth and having high proportion of poor. In states like *Kerala, Karnataka* and *West Bengal*, the problem of poverty is very acute despite relatively more progressive and better implemented land reform laws.

Similarly, more irrigation facilities have failed to guarantee better life to the poor in *U.P.* Development of institutional credit facilities may be a great help in tackling the problem but in the absence of proper structural changes, they fail to solve the problem as is clear from the experience of *Eastern Plains of West Bengal, Coastal and Southern Orissa and Coastal Ghats of Karnataka and Maharashtra.* It is thus clear that the macro level controversy of institutional-structural changes versus technocratic approach is completely out of focus.

Egalitarian land reform policies have also not succeeded equally in all regions as is reflected in the highly differentiated land deprivation pattern in the regions.

The perusal of the poverty and structural profiles of regions makes it abundantly clear that ownership of land is not the main problem of poverty in many regions in which average value of land is high and concentration is low. However, because of low level of infrastructure development and other problems, the poverty situation is no less serious. Such is the situation in *Western M.P., dry areas of Gujarat, Northern Plains of Gujarat and Saurashtra.* To a lesser extent this is also true of *Eastern Plains of Maharashtra, South Rajasthan* and *Western M.P.* They and all of *Maharashtra* suffer from low productivity.

In states like *Bihar* and *Orissa* and to lesser extent in States *other than Punjab* and *Haryana*, the bargaining power of the poor sections of the population in the land, labour, credit and product markets is very weak and since the markets are interlocked, the exploitation of the poor is not limited by an social or economic consideration. Hence the task of prime importance in almost all states should be to increase the bargaining power of these sections in these markets and to reduce the control of the inter-penetrating markets by the stronger sections of the population. Since concentration of land and other assets is very high in almost all regions and most of credit to the weaker sections is controlled by the moneylenders, traders and landlords, this hold is difficult to loosen until fundamental structural changes are undertaken. Hence, even if effective land reforms directed towards more equitable distribution of land and other assets are not a sufficient condition for removal of poverty, they are a necessary condition.

An important factor in the poverty situation is that the poor are not only economically deprived but are also politically isolated and unorganised and are, thus, victims of caste, ethnic-tribal and linguistic discrimination, and political and police oppression.

Alongwith the structural changes, institutional agencies for the poor should be further strengthened. Scale and class neutral infrastructure development like major irrigation projects and scale and class neutral technologies (like new seeds, new crops) and inputs (like green and compost manure) should be developed. This requires changing the strategy of agricultural development hitherto adopted. It is, again, to be noted that special programmes for specific regions or problems (Tribal, Desert, Hill development) or specific sections of the poor (Small farmers, marginal farmers, agricultural labourers, scheduled castes and tribes) can be successful in removing absolute poverty without increasing relative poverty only if the above structural changes take place. The converse is not necessarily true. And the experience of many non-socialist developing countries shows that these structural changes are politically feasible within the existing political systems and are also economically desirable.

It should be noted that the economic condition of the poor may not improve substantially in many parts of the country despite all the required land reforms and changes in the agrarian development strategy. This may be because of the population pressure as in *Kerala, West Bengal, Eastern U.P., Coastal A.P.*, and much of *Tamil Nadu* or adverse geophysical conditions such as in *Western Rajasthan*, parts of *Karnataka, A.P.*, and *Maharashtra*. Rapid development of the non-agricultural sector is, therefore, necessary. In other states also, this will be helpful in reducing pressure on agriculture and in providing the necessary inputs.

Feminisation of poverty and ecological marginalisation of the poor are also going to pose new problems in the future. Appropriate policies have to be directed towards tackling these problems in such a way that the economic position of the poor is not further eroded in the name of preservation of environment and conservation of resources. For guaranteeing this too, effective institutional changes and land reforms are urgently required.

BIBLIOGRAPHY

Adams, John and Baloo Bumb (1973). The economic and political social dimension of an Indian State : An factor analysis of district data for Rajasthan, *Journal of Asian Studies*, XXXIII (1), Nov.

Adelman, Irma and George Dalton (1971). Factor analysis of modernization in village India, in George Dalton (Ed). *Economic Anthropology and Development : Essays on Tribal and Peasant Economies.* New York, Basic Books : 304-25.

——, and Cynthia Morris Taft (1971). Analysis of variance techniques for the study of economic development, *Journal of Development Studies*, VIII October : 93-94.

——, and C.T. Morris (1967). *Society, Politics and Economic Growth.* John Hopkins University, Baltimore.

——, and Subbarao, K., Vashistha, Prem (1985). Some dynamic aspects of rural poverty in India, *EPW, Review of Agriculture*, XX (39) September 28.

Ahluwalia, Montek S. (1977). *Rural Poverty and Growth in Indian Agriculture.* Development Research Centre, The World Bank, Washington, DC, June.

——, (1978), Rural poverty in India : 1956-57 to 1973-74. *World Bank Staff Working Paper* (279), May.

——, (1978). Rural poverty and agricultural performance in India, *Journal of Development Studies*, XIV (3) : 298-323.

Agrawal, Bina (1986). Women and agricultural growth in India. *Journal of Peasant Studies* XIII (1–).

Ahluwalia, M.S., Carters, N.G., Chenery, H.B., and Development Staff (1979). Growth and poverty in developing countries, *World Bank Staff Working Paper* (309) (Revised), Washington.

Ahluwalia, M.S. (1986). Rural poverty, agricultural production and prices : A reexamination. In: Mellor and Desai (Eds.) (1986): 59-75.

AIDIS, 1981-82 (1987). *All India Debt and Investment Survey: Assets and Liabilities as on 30th June 1981*, Reserve Bank of India, Bombay.

AIRDIS, 1971-72. *Statistical Tables Relating to Cash Dues Outstanding Against Rural Households as on 30th June 1971*, R.B.I. Bombay.

——. *Statistical Tables Relating to Capital Expenditure and Capital Formation*, R.B.I., Bombay.

All India Rural Debt Survey, 1958-59.

Andrews, F.M. (1974). Social indicators of perceived life quality, *Social Indicators Research* I: 279-299.

Athreya, V. et al (1987). Identification of agrarian classes : A methodological essay with empirical material from South India, *The Journal of Peasant Studies*, XIV (2), Jan: 147-190.

Atkinson, A.B. (1970). On the measurement of inequality, *Journal of Economic Theory*, 23(2) : 244-263.

——, (1975). The economics of inequality. Oxford Clarendorn Press.

Bardhan, Pranab K. (1970). Trends in land relations. *EPW*, V. Jan.

—— (1982, 1986). Poverty and trickle down in rural India: A quantitative analysis. *Working Paper, University of Californian, Berkeley.* Also in: Mellor and Desai (1986): 76-94.

——, (1984). *Land Labour and Rural Poverty.* Oxford University Press.

——, (1983). Regional variations in the rural economy, *EPW*, XVII(30).

——, (1987). Poverty and employment characteristics of urban households in West Bengal. *EPW*, XXII(35), Aug. 29:1502, fn 2.

Bardhan P. and Ashok Rudra (1980). Type of labour attachment in agriculture. *EPW*, X(35), Aug : 1477.

Berg (1973). The Nutrition factor. Brookings, D. :293.

Beteille, A., (1974). *Studies in Agrarian Social Structure.* O.U. Press, New Delhi.

Bhaduri, Amit (1973). A study in agricultural backwardness under semi-feudalism. *Economic Journal.* 83(329) March : 120-137.

Bhalla, G.S. and Y.K. Alagh (1979). *Performance of Indian Agriculture : A District Wise Study.* Sterling Publishers, New Delhi.

——, (1987). *Agrarian Structure, Land Reforms and Agricultural Growth in India.* CRD, JNU, New Delhi (mimeo).

Bhattacharya, N. et al. (1980). Regional price indices based on NSS 28th round consumer expenditure survey data. *Sarvekshana,* III(4) : 107-121.

——, (1985). *On Variation in Level of Living Across Regions and Social Groups During* 1963-64 — 1973-74, Social Science Division, I.S.I., Calcutta. (mimeo)

Bhattacharya, N. et al., (1985). *Disparities of Living Across States and Social Groups During* 1973-74. Social Science Division, I.S.T., Calcutta.

Bhatty, I.Z. and M.T.R. Sarma (1977). Saving behaviour in India an implications for poverty in : C.D. Wadhwa (ed) (1977).

Booth, C. (1889). *Life and Labour of the People in London.* London.

Breman, J. (1974). *Patronage and exploitation; Changing agrarian social relations in South Gujarat.* University of California Press, Berkeley.

Chakravarty, S.R. (1983). A new index of poverty. *Mathematical Social Sciences.* VI,: 307-313.

Chakravarty, S.R. and M. Panda (1981). Measurement of incidence of undernutrition, *EPW*, XVI, (31), Aug.

Chatterjee, G.S. and Bhattacharya N. (1974). On disparities in per capita household consumption in India. In: T.N. Srinivasan and P.K. Bardhan (eds.) (1984) and *Sankhya, C*, 36 (2 and 4) : 183-214.

——, (1974a). Between states variation in consumer prices and per capita household consumption in India, *Sankhya, C,* 36 (2 and 4): 351-368.

Chattopadhyaya, Paresh (1972). On the question of mode of production of Indian agriculture. *EPW*, VII, Review of Agriculture, Pune.

Coelen, S.P. (1980). Regression analysis of regional quality of life, *Social Indicators Research,* VIII : 467-479.

Coelen, S.P. and Nakosteen, Robert A. (1981). Quality of life as a framework for a simultaneous socio-economic and demographic model. *Population Association of America, Annual Conference,* March.

Cramer, J.S. (1968). *Empirical Econometrics*, North Holland Publishing Co: 145-151.

Dandekar V.M. and Nilakantha Rath (1971). *Poverty in India*, Indian School of Political Economy : 124-126.

——, (1971). Poverty in India. *Economic and Political Weekly,* VI(1,2) Jan.

Dandekar, V.M. (1981). On measurement of poverty, *EPW,* XVI(30) July : 1241-50.

——, (1982). On measurement of undernutrition. *EPW,* XVIII(6) Feb.

Dantwala, M.L. (1973, 1974). *Poverty in India, Then and Now,* 1978-1980. Macmillan.

——, (1973). *Poverty and Unemployment in India.* Report on a Project, 65-66.

—— (1976), Social dimensions of poverty. *Vishleshan* II(2), July.

——, (1986). Technology, growth and equity in agriculture. In: Mellor and Desai (eds.) (1986): 110-123.

——, (1987). Rural asset distribution and composition of labour force, *IJAE,* 42(3), July : 275-285.

Dasgupta, Biplab (1971). Socio economic classification of districts, a statistical approach. *Economic and Political Weekly,* VI, Aug. : 1763-1773.

Dasgupta P. and D. Roy (1986). *Adopting to Undernourishment. The Clinical Evidence and Its Implications.* Discussion Paper No. 106, Department of Applied Economics, Cambridge.

Erikson, R. et al (1985). *The Scandinavian Model, Welfare State and Welfare Research.* New York, M.E. Sharpe.

Fields, Gray S. (1980). *Poverty, Inequality and Development.* New York, Cambridge University Press.

——, (1989) Changes in poverty and inequality in developing countries. *The World Bank Research Observer,* IV, 2 8 (July).

Fitzsimmons, S.J. and W.G. Lavey (1976). Social economic accounting system : Towards a comprehensive community-level assessment procedure. *Social Indicators Research,* II : 389-452.

F.A.O. (1973). *Energy and Protein Requirements. Report of a Joint* FAO-WHO Expert Committee. FAO, Rome.

Foster-Carter, A. (1978). The modes of production controversy. *New Left Review,* 107 : 47-77.

Foster, J., Greer J. and E. Thorbecke (1984). A class of decomposable poverty measures, *Econometrica,*, 52(3).

Frankel, Francine (1978). *Indian Political Economy (1947-1978).* Oxford University Press : 78.

Fructher, Benjamin (1967). *Introduction to Factor Analysis.* D. Van Nustrand Co, East-West Edition, New Delhi.

Gaiha, R and M. Kazmi (1981). Aspects of poverty in rural India, *Economics of Planning,* XVII (2-3) : 74-112.

Ganguli, B.N. and D.B. Gupta (1976). *Levels of Living in India.* S.Chand and Co., New Delhi.

Ghai, Dharma et al (eds.) (1979). *Agrarian Systems and Rural Development.* Holmes and Meier Pub. Inc., New York. : 72:108.

Ginsberg, N. (Ed.) (1960). *Essays on Geography and Economic Development.* Chicago University Press.

Greer, J. and E. Thorbecke (1986). Food poverty profile applied to Kenyan small-holders. *Economic Development and Cultural Change,* XXX (1) Oct. : 117-140.

Griffin, K. and A.K. Ghosh (1979). Growth and impoverishment in the rural areas of Asia. *World Development,* I (4/5).

Guhan, S. (1980). Rural poverty : Policy and play acting. *EPW,* XV (47), Nov. 22.

Gupta, Deepankar (1980). Formal and real sumsumption of labour by capital, the instance of share-cropping. *EPW, Review of Agriculture,* XV, Sept. : A98-A102.

Gutkind, E. (1983). *Towards Basic Needs Policies in Development Planning.* I.L.O. WEP 2-32/wp 47, Jan.

—— (1986). *Patterns of Economic Behaviour Among the American Poor.* St. Martin's Press, New York.

Ghosh, A. and K. Dutt (1977). *Development of Capitalist Mode of Production in Agriculture.* Peoples Publishing House, Delhi, July : 85-86.

Harman, H.H. (1960). *Modern Factor Analysis.* Chicago, Chicago University Press.

Harriss, John (1987). *Capitalism and Peasant Farming : Agrarian Structure and Ideology in Northern Tamil Nadu.* O.U. Press, Bombay.

Hicks, J.R. (1940). Valuation of social income. *Review of Economic Studies,* VII.

—— (1958). Measurement of real income. *Oxford Economic Papers,* X.

Hicks, H. (1982). Sector priorities meeting basic needs : Some statistical evidence. *World Development,* X (6).

Heston, A.W. (1980). *Regional Economic Development in South Asia : Recent Developments, Some Historical Perspectives.* University of Pennsylvania, Mimeographed : 22-23.

Hoch, Irving (1977). *Public Economics and the Quality of Life*. The John Hopkins University Press, Baltimore, Maryland.

India, Govt. of (1981). *Sixth Five Year Plan Framework* : 30.

—— (undated). *Report of the Task Force on Agrarian Relations*. Delhi : 6.7.

India, Govt. of (G.O.I.) (1978). *Draft Five Year Plan, 1978-1983.* : 98.

—— (1985). *Report of the Committee to Review Existing Arrangements of Rural Development and Poverty Alleviation Programmes*. Department of Rural Development, Dec.

Indian National Nutrition Monitoring Bureau (1981). *Report for the Year (1980)*. National Institute of Nutrition, ICMR, Hyderabad.

I.L.O. (1976). *Employment, Growth and Basic Needs*. Geneva. I.L.O.

—— (1986). *Fighting Poverty : Asia's Major Challenge*. I.L.O., Asian Employment Programme, New Delhi.

Iyengar, N.S. and M.H. Suryanarayan (1984). On poverty indicators. *Economic and Political Weekly*, XIX (22&23), June.

Jain, L.R., K. Sundaram and S.O. Tendulkar (1988). Dimensions of rural poverty : An inter-regional profile. *EPW*, XXIII (Nov.) 2395-2408.

Jain, T.L. (1987). *Poverty in India*. ESS Publications, New Delhi.

James, William E., Naya, Seiji and G.M. Meier (1988). *Asian Development Success and Policy Lessions*. University of Wisconsin Press, Madison.

Johnston, J. (1972). *Econometric Methods*. Second edition. McGraw-Hill, New York.

Johar, R.S. and P. Singh (1981). On poverty in India. *PSE Economic Analyst X*, Guru Nanak Dev University, Amritsar. May-June : 118-147.

Joshi, P.C. (1978). Evaluation of land reforms. In: Charan D. Wadhwa (ed.). *Some Problems of Indian Economic Policy* : 448-450.

Kakwani, Nanak (1978). *Income Inequality and Poverty, Methods of Estimation and Policy Applications*. World Bank, Washington, D.C.

—— (1980). on a class of poverty measures, *Econometrica*, XLVII : 437-46.

—— (1980). *Income Inequality and Poverty*. Oxford University Press.

—— (1986). *On Measuring Undernutrition*. World Institute for Development Economics Research, Helsinki (mimeo).

Krishnaji, N. (1987). Agricultural growth, prices and rural poverty. *EPW*, XXII (26), June.

Kundu, Amitabh (1980). *Measurement of Urban Processes : A Study in Regionalisation*. Bombay, Popular Prakashan.

—— (1981). Measurement of poverty — Some conceptual issues. *Anvesak*, XI (1-2), Sardar Patel Institute of Economic and Social Research.

Kundu, A. and T.E. Smith (1983). An impossibility theorem on poverty indices. *International Economic Review*, XXIV (2) : 423.

Kurien, C.T. (1977). *Poverty and Development*. The Christian Literary Society.

Lakdawala, D.T. (1977, 1978). Growth, unemployment and poverty. Presidential Address, All India Labour Economics Conference Tirupati, also *Indian Journal of Labour Economics*, Ap.–July, 1978.

—— (1979). *Forces of Growth*. Commerce Publication Division, Bombay.

Lanjouw, Peter and Nicholos Stern (1991). Poverty in Palanpur, *The World Bank Economic Review*, V (1), Jan : 23-56.

Larson, David A. and Welford, Walton, T. (1980). The physical quality of life index. A new measure of welfare. *Indian Economic Journal*, XXVII (3), Jan.-March.

Lipton, Michael (1977). *Why Poor People Stay Poor. Urban Bias in World Development*. London : Temple Smith.

—— (1983a). *Poverty, Undernutrition, and Hunger*. World Bank Staff Working Papers, No. 579.

—— (1983b). *Labour and Poverty*. World Bank Staff Working Papers, No. 616.

Liu, B.C. (1970). *The Quality of Life in the United States*. Kansas city, MO: Mid-West Research Institute.

—— (1975). Quality of life: Concept, measure and results. *American Journal of Economics and Sociology*, XXXIV : 396-405.

—— (1980). Economic growth and quality of life. *American Journal of Economics and Sociology*, XXXIX : 1-21.

Mahendra Dev S. (1986). Growth of labour productivity in Indian agriculture: Regional dimensions. *Economic and Political Weekly*, XXI, June : 21-28.

Mather, P.M. (1976). *Computational Methods of Multivariate Analysis in Physical Geography*. John Wiley and Sons.

McLaren, D. (1974). *The Great Protein Fiasco*. The Lancet : 2.

Mehta, B.C. (1978). *Regional Population Growth*. Research Books, Jaipur.

—— (1978). Structure of Rajasthan's economy — An Input-Output analysis. *ICSSR Research Abstracts* VII (4), Oct.-Dec.

—— (1979). Rural economy of Rajasthan. *National Labour Institute Bulletin*, V (3-4), March-April.

—— (1980). Antyodaya : An appraisal. *Rajasthan Economic Journal*, III (2), July.

—— (1983). *Structure of Rajasthan's Economy*. Research Books, Jaipur, 2nd Ed. Malkani Book Agency, Udaipur, 1986.

Mehta, B.C. (1984). Administration of minimum wages in remote agricultural areas. *National Labour Institute Bulletin*. X (1-2), Jan.-June : 22-37.

—— (1990). A study of rural poverty and its correlates in Indian states in early seventies and early eighties. *Indian Journal of Regional Science*, XXII (1) : 59-74.

Mehta, B.C. and N.L. Hatharia (1975). Regional imbalances in Rajasthan's development. *Economic Times*, Dec. 5, 6.

Mehta, B.C. and Avadh Prashad (1980). Case studies of exploitation in Rajasthan. *National Labour Institute Bulletin*, VI (3-4), March-April.

—— (1988). *Agrarian Relations and Rural Exploitation*. Ashish Publishing House, Delhi.

Mehta, B.C. and Ashok Khandelwal (1981). *Structure of Rural Economy of Rajasthan*. Rajasthan Peoples Publishing House, Jaipur.

Mehta, B.C. and Kumud Dave (1987). Disparities in regional development. In: A.C. Angrish (ed.) *Regional Economic Planning in India*. Twenty First Century Publishers, Meerut.

Mellor, John W. and Gunwant Desai (eds.) (1986). *Agricultural Change and Rural Poverty: Variations on a Theme by Dharam Narain*. Oxford University Press, Delhi.

Mencher, J.P. (1982). Agricultural labourers and poverty. *EPW*, XVII (1&2), Jan. : 38.

Merton, R.K. (1987). *Social Theory and Social Structure*. (Rev. Edn.), Glenco, Illinois, Free Press.

Minhas, B.S. (1970). Rural poverty, land redistribution and development. *Indian Economic Review*, April.

—— (1974, 1976). *Planning and the Poor*. S. Chand and Company : 63-101.

Mishra, G.P. (ed.) (1985). *Regional Structure of Development and Growth in India. I & II.* Ashish Publishing House, Delhi.

Morris, M.D. (1979). *Measuring the Condition of the World's Poor: The Physical Quality of Life Index.* Oxford Pergamon Press.

Morris, M.D. and McAlpin, M.B. (1982). *Measuring the Economic Condition of India's Poor: The Physical Quality of Life Index.* Promilla and Co., New Delhi.

Mundle, Sundip (1983). Effects of agricultural production and prices on incidence of poverty. A A tentative analysis of inter-state variation. *EPW*, XVIII (26), June.

National Council of Applied Economic Research (NCAER) (1986). *Changes in Poverty and Consumption Pattern in Rural India between 1970-71—1981-82 : Longitudinal Analysis.* New Delhi (Mimeo).

National Institute of Nutrition (India) (1976). *Annual Report 1975.* Indian Council of Medical Research, Hyderabad.

National Nutrition Monitoring Bureau (India) (1979). *Report for the Year 1978.* Hyderabad.

—— (1981). *Report for the Year 1980.* Hyderabad.

Oshima, P. (1988). Income distribution in Asia: A brief comparative review. In: S. Ichimura (ed.) *Developing Strategies and Productivity Issues in Asia.* Tokyo, 1988.

Pal, Padmaja, S.R. Chakravarty and N. Bhattacharya (1985). *Poverty in Rural India: A Decomposition Analysis.* Indian Statistical Institute, Calcutta. Tech. Report No. ERU/6/85, July.

Panda, N.K. (1986). Fixing income and price targets for the poor in India. *Journal of Development Economics*, XX (2).

—— (1987). Poverty in rural Orissa (1960-83). *Margin*, XX (2), oct.-Dec. : 42-45.

Panikar, P.G.K. (1972). Economics of nutrition, *Economic and Political Weekly*, VII, Annual Number, Feb. : 413-430.

—— (1978). Employment, income and food intake among selected agricultural labour households. *Economic and Political Weekly*, XIII (31, 32 & 33), Special Number, Aug. : 1367-1372.

Parthasarathy, G. (1978). *Interstate Variation of Rural Unemployment and Growth of Agriculture.* Agroeconomic Research Centre, Andhra University Waltair.

—— (1982). Rural poverty and female heads of households : Needs for quantitative analysis. *Seminar paper*, Institute of Social Studies Trust, April, 9-11.

—— (1984). Land, labour and poverty. *Economic and Political Weekly*, XIX (50), Dec.

—— (1986). Presidential Address, 46th Annual Conference of the Indian Society of Agricultural Economics, Udaipur, Dec. Also published in *IJAE*.

—— (1986). Dharam Narain's Approach to rural poverty. In: Mellor and Desai (eds.) (1986) : 181-185.

Pathak, R.P., Ganapathy, K.R. and Sarma, Y.U.K. (1977). Shift in pattern of asset holdings of rural households, 1961-62 to 1971-72, *EPW*, XII, March.

Patnaik, Utsa (1972). On the mode of production in Indian agriculture. *EPW*, VII, Review of Agriculture, Dec. : A145-151.

—— (1976). Differentiation within peasantry. *EPW*, *Review of Agriculture*, Sept.

—— (1976). Class differentiation within the peasantry : An approach to the analysis of Indian Agriculture. *EPW*, XI (39), *Review of Agriculture* : 82-101.

—— (1978). Development of capitalism in agriculture. In: *Studies in the Development of Capitalism in India*, Lahore, Vanguard Books, 1978.

—— (1980). Empirical identification of peasant classes revisited. *EPW*, XV (9) : 438.

—— (1990) (Ed.). *Agrarian Relations and Accumulation*. Oxford University Press, Bombay.

Perspective Planning Division (1962). Perspective of development 1961-1976, implications of planning for minimum level of living. In: Srinivasan and Bardhan (eds.) (1974).

—— (1979). *Report of the Taskforce in Projecting of Minimum Needs and Effective Consumption Demand*. Planning Commission, Govt. of India, New Delhi.

Pidot Jr., G.S. (1969). A principal components analysis of determinants of local Government fiscal patterns. *Rev. of Economics and Statistics*, LI.

Planning Commission (1978). *Draft Five Year Plan 1978-83.* : 50.

—— (1979). *Sixth Five Year Plan, 1978-83.* : 37.

—— (1981). *A Technical Note on the Sixth Five Year Plan of India (1980-85)*. G.O.I., New Delhi.

—— (1981). *Sixth Five Year Plan, 1980-85.* : 51.

Pradhan, H. S. Prashad (1973). Production relations, achille's heels of Indian Planning. *EPW*, VIII, May, 19.

—— (1976). Poverty and bondage, *EPW*, XI, Special Number, Aug.

—— (1979). Caste and class in Bihar, *EPW*, XI, Feb.

—— (1985). Poverty and agriculture development. *EPW*, XX (50), Dec.

Raj Krishna (1980). Income, poverty, unemployment. *Economic Times*, May, 10.

Ranade, Sudhanshu (1988). On estimating and explaining rural poverty. *EPW*, XXIII (16), April : 805-808.

R.B.I., See AIDIS.

Rao, C.H. Hanumantha, S.P. Gupta, K.L. Dutta (1985). Poverty eradication in India by the year 2000. Some macro-economic implications. *Man and Development*, Dec. : 29-37.

Rao, C.H. Hanumantha, D.B. Gupta and P.S. Sharma (1986). Infrastructural development and rural poverty : A cross-sectional analysis. In: Mellor and Desai (eds.) : 95-109.

Rao, M. (1979). Nutrition situation in India during 1971-72, *Sarvekshana*, III (4), Jan.

Rao, R.S. (1970). In search of capitalist farmer, *EPW*, V, Dec.

Ravallion, Martin and Monika Huppi (1991). Measuring changes in poverty. A methodological case study of Indonesia, *The World Bank Economic Review*, V (1), Jan. : 57-84.

Rawls, John (1971). *A Theory of Justice*. Cambridge, Mass, Harvard University Press.

Raza, M. and A. Kundu (1980). *Regional Disparities in India*. Centre for Regional Development, Jawaharlal Nehru University (ICSSR Project).

Reddy, K.N. (1976). Inter-state difference in social consumption. *EPW*, XI, June, 12 : 872-879.

Research and Planning Division of the ESCAPE Secretariat (1972). On the measurement of mass poverty in India. *Economic Bulletin for Asia and Far East*. XXIII (3).

Reutlinger, S. and M. Selowsky (1976). *Malnutrition and Poverty*. World Bank Occasional Paper No. 23, Washington DC.

Ringen, Stein (1985). Toward a third stage in the measurement of poverty. *Acta Sociologica*, XXVIII (2) : 99-113.

—— (1988). Direct and indirect measures of poverty. *Journal of Social Policy*, XVII (3) : 351-365.

Rouch and Rouch. *Poverty*, Penguin Books, Introduction : 25-26.

Rowntree, B.S. (1901). *Poverty : A Study of Town Life*. London. Macmillan.

Roy, B.K. (1986). Agricultural typology in India: Some issues. In: Singh and Singh (eds.) (1986) : 149-157.

Rudra, Ashok (1974). Minimum level of living — A statistical examination. In: T.N. Srinivasan and P.K. Bardhan (eds.): *Poverty and Income Distribution in India*. Statistical Publishing Society, Calcutta.

—— (1978). Class relations in India's agriculture. *EPW*, XIII, June, 3 & 7.

Rudra, Ashok (1979). Organisation of agriculture for rural development. In: Dharam Ghai (ed.) *Agrarian Systems and Rural Development*. Holmes and Meier publishers : 72-108.

Runciman, W.G. (1966). *Relative Deprivation and Social Justice*, London, Routledge and Kegan Paul.

Sagar, Sushma, K. Ahuja and Vidya Sagar (1987). Poverty among identified weaker sections in Rajasthan. *EPW*, XXII.

Saith, Ashwani (1981). Production, price and poverty in India. *The Journal of Development Studies*, XVII (2), January.

Sanyal, S.K. (1977). Trend in some characteristics of land-holdings. *Sarvekshana*, I (1), July.

—— (1984). Agricultural productivity, unemployment and landholdings structure. Some tentative hypotheses. *Economic and Political Weekly*, XIX, (52 & 53), *Review of Agriculture,* Dec., 22, & 29 : A-179-188.

Sarvekshana (1983). Per capita per diem intake of nutrients. NSS, 27th round. *Sarvekshana*, VI (3-4), April: S-1 to S-88.

Sastry, S.A.R. (1980). A Survey of literature on poverty, income distribution and development. *Artha Vijnana*, XXII, (1), March : 82.

Sastry, S.A.R. and T. Suryanarayana (1981). Optimum diet and poverty line. In: *Employment Poverty and Public Policy*. ed. by Sardar Patel Institute of Economic and Social Research, Ahmedabad, Allied Publishers, New Delhi : 97-116.

Sau, Ranjit (1971). On rural poverty — A tentative hypothesis, *EPW*, VI, Dec., 25.

—— (1976). Can capitalism develop in Indian agriculture? *EPW*, XI, *Review of Agriculture*, Dec.

—— (1978a). Growth, employment and removal of poverty. *EPW*, XII, (31, 32 & 33), Special Number.

—— (1978b). *Unequal Exchange : An Essay on the Political Economy of World Capitalism*. Oxford University Press, Calcutta.

—— (1978c). Class relations in Indian agriculture. *EPW*, XIII (23, 24, 25).

—— (1980). Indian economic crisis: A reply. *EPW*, XV (16), April, 19.

Scandizzo, P. and Knudsen, O. (1979). *Nutrition and Food Needs of Developing Countries*. World Bank Staff Papers, No. 328.

Scanlon, T.M. (1975). Preference and urgency. *Journal of Philosophy*, LXXII.

Sen, A.K. (1973). Poverty inequality and unemployment. Some conceptual issues in measurement. *Economic and Political Weekly*, VIII, Special Number, August. Reprinted in, Srinivasan and Bardhan (eds.) (1974).

—— (1973). *On Economic Inequality*. Oxford, Clarendon Press.

—— (1973). On the development of basic economic indicators to supplement GNP measures, *United Nations Economic Bulletin for Asia and the Far East* 24.

—— (1975, 77). Poverty and economic development. The 2nd Vikram Sarabhai Memorial Lecture, 1975. Also published in Charan Wadhwa (ed.) *Some Problems of India Economic Policy*, 1977 : 241-253.

—— (1980). *Levels of Poverty, Policy and Change*. World Bank Staff Working Paper No. 401.

—— (1982, 1983). *Choice, Welfare and Measurement*. Oxford University Press, Delhi : 353-372. Reprint of original published by Oxford University Press, 1983.

Sen, Amartya and Sunil Sengupta (1983). Malnutrition rural children and the sex bias, *Economic and Political Weekly*, XVII (19, 20 & 21), Annual Number : 855-64.

Shanin, Teodor (1977). Measuring peasant capitalism: Russia's 1920s and India's 1970s. *EPW*, XII (47) : 1939-48.

Sheldon, E.B. and Freeman, H.E. (1970). Notes on social indicators. Promises and Potential. *Policy Science*, I : 97-111.

Sharma, D.P. (1985). Explaining poverty. *Margin*, XVII (2), Jan.

Sharma, K.L. (1975). Spatial disparities in Rajasthan. *Indian Journal of Regional Science*, VII (1) : 88-98.

—— (1987). Agrarian stratification : old issues, new explanations. *EPW*, XVIII (42, 43), Oct. 15, 22 : 1796-1803, 1951-1955.

Singh, Tarlok (1988). Agriculture and rural poverty: Issues reexamined. *ICSSR Newsletter*, XIX (1), April-June, 1-18.

Singh, V.R. and N.K. Singh (1986). An appraisal of the typological classification of agriculture in India. In Singh, V.R. and N.K. Singh (eds.) : 74-78.

—— (Eds.) (1986). *Perspectives in Agricultural Typology*, Varanasi, Star Distributors.

Sinha, R.P. Pearson, G. Kadekodi (1979). *Income Distribution, Growth and Basic Needs in India*. Vikas Publishing House : 27-29.

Smith, T. and A. Kundu (1983). See Kundu, A. and T. Smith (1983).

Srinivasan, T.N. and P.K. Bardhan (ed.), 1974). *Poverty and Income Distribution in India*. Statistical Publishing Society, Calcutta.

Srinivasan, T.N. (1979). *Malnutrition : Some Measurement and Policy Issues* (mimeographed). World Bank and Yale University.

—— (1986). Agricultural production, relative prices, entitlements, and poverty. In: Mellor and Desai (1986).

Stone, R. (1960). A comparison of the economic structures of regions based on the concept of 'distance'. *Journal of Regional Science*, II.

Streetan, P. (1981). *First Things First: Meeting Mass Human Needs in Developing Countries*. New York, O.U.P.

Subrahmanyam, S. (1982). Poverty, unemployment and labour force participation. *Margin*, XV (1) Oct.

Sukhatme, P.V. (1973). The calorie gap. *The Indian Journal of Nutrition and Dietetics*, X (198).

—— (1977). *Malnutrition and Poverty*. Ninth L.B. Shastri Memorial Lecture, Indian Agricultural Research Institute, New Delhi.

—— (1978). Assessment of adequacy of diets at different income levels, *Economic and Political Weekly*, XIII (31-33) : 1373.

—— (1980). Nutrition policy: Need for reorientation, *EPW*, XV (26), June.

—— (1981a). Measuring the incidence of under-nutrition: A comment. *EPW*, XVI (23), : 1034-6.

—— (1981b). On measurement of poverty. *EPW*, XVI (32), Aug. : 1318-24.

—- (1982). Measurement of undernutrition. *EPW*, XVII (50) Dec.

—— (ed.) (1982). *New Concepts in Nutrition and Their Implications for Policy*. Maharashtra Association for the Cultivation of Science, Pune.

Takayama, N. (1979). Poverty income inequality and their measures: Professor Sen's approach reconsidered. *Econometrica*, XLVII (2) : 747-59.

Thakur, D.S. (1985). A survey of literature on rural poverty in India. *Margin*, XVIII, April : 32 to 49.

—— (1986). Estimation of poverty in India — An empirical investigation. *Margin*, XIX 19 (1) Oct.

Thon, D. (1979). On measuring poverty. *Review of Income and Wealth*, XXV (4).

Thorner, Alice (1982). Semi-feudalism or capitalism? Contemporary debate on classes and mode of production in India. *EPW*, XVII (49, 50, 51), Dec.

Titmus, R. (1962). *Income Distribution and Social Change*. London, George Allen Unwin.

Townsend, P. (Ed.) (1970). *The Concept of Poverty*. London, Heinemann, HEB paperback.

—— (1974). Poverty as relative deprivation: Resources and style of living. In: Dorothy Wedderburn (ed.) *Poverty, Inequality and Class*. Cambridge Uni. Press : 15-41.

Tyagi, S.S. and Laxminarayan, H. (1976). Some aspects of size distribution of agricultural holdings, *EPW*, XV, Oct. : 1637-1640.

Tyagi, D.S. (1982). How valid are the estimates of trends in rural poverty. *EPW*, XVII, June, *Review of Agriculture* : 54-62.

—— (1985). Trends in rural poverty and distrust of growth: some methodological issues. In: G.D. Mishra (ed.) *Regional Structure of Development and Growth in India*. Volume I : 239.

United Nations (1975). *Poverty, Unemployment and Development Policy — A Case Study of Selected Issues with Reference to Kerala*. New York : Department of Economic and Social Affairs, United Nations (ST/ESA/29).

U.N.O. (1954). *International Definition and Measurement of Standards and Level of Living*.

—— (1972). On the measurement of mass poverty in India. *Economic Bulletin for Asia and the Far East*, XXII (93).

Uusitalo, H. (1975). *Income and Welfare*. Research Group for Comparative Sociology, University of Helsinki.

Vaidyanathan, A. (1974). Some aspects of inequalities in living standards in rural India. In: Srinivasan and Bardhan (eds.) *Poverty and Income Distribution in India*. Statistical Publishing Society, Calcutta : 215-241.

Visaria, Leela (1985). Infant mortality in India: Levels, trends and determinants. *EPW*, XX (33, 34), Aug. 17 : 1400-1403, 1449.

Visaria, Parvin (1974). Labour force unemployment and underemployment in India : Retrospect an Prospect. In: J.C. Sandesara (ed.) *The Indian Economy : Performance and Prospects*. Bombay, University of Bombay.

—— (1980). Poverty and unemployment in India. *Indian Journal of Agricultural Economics*, July-Sept.

—— (1981). *Size of Land-holding, Living Standards and Employment in Rural Western India, 1972-73*. World Bank Staff Working Paper No. 459, May.

Visaria, P. and L. Visaria (1983). Indian households with female heads: Their incidence, characteristics and level of living. Paper presented at a workshop on *Women and Poverty*, Center for Studies in Social Sciences, Calcutta, 17-18 March.

Vyas, N.N. (1980). *Bondage and Exploitation in Tribal India*. Rawat Publications, Jaipur.

Wadhava, C.D. (1977). *Some Problem of India's Economic Policy*. Tata McGraw-Hill, New Delhi.

INDEX